BRITISH FOREIGN AND IMPERIAL POLICY, 1865–1919

QUESTIONS AND ANALYSIS IN HISTORY

Edited by Stephen J. Lee, Sean Lang and Jocelyn Hunt

Other titles in this series:

BRITISH FOREIGN AND IMPERIAL POLICY, 1865–1919

GRAHAM D. GOODLAD

ROUTLEDGE

London and New York

First published 2000 by Routledge
11 New Fetter Lane, London EC4P 4EE

Simultaneously published in the USA and Canada
by Routledge
29 West 35th Street, New York, NY 10001

Routledge is an imprint of the Taylor & Francis Group

Typeset in Grotesque and Perpetua
by Keystroke, Jacaranda Lodge, Wolverhampton
Printed and bound in Great Britain by MPG Books Ltd, Bodmin

British Library Cataloguing in Publication Data
A catalogue record for this book is available from the British Library

Library of Congress Cataloging in Publication Data
Goodlad, Graham D. (Graham David), 1964–
    British foreign and imperial policy, 1865–1919 / Graham D.
Goodlad.
       p.   cm. – (Questions and analysis in history)
    Includes blbiographical references and index.
       1. Great Britain–Foreign relations–1837–1901. 2. Imperialism–
Government policy–Great Britain–History–19th century.
    3. Imperialism–Government policy–Great Britain–History–20th
century. 4. Great Britain–Foreign relations–1901–1936.
    I. Title. II. Series.
    DA560.G66   1999
    327.41–dc21   99-15660
                                                 CIP

ISBN 0–415–20338–4

CONTENTS

SERIES PREFACE

Most history textbooks now aim to provide the student with interpretation, and many also cover the historiography of a topic. Some include a selection of sources.

So far, however, there have been few attempts to combine *all* the skills needed by the history student. Interpretation is usually found within an overall narrative framework and it is often difficult to separate out the two for essay purposes. Where sources are included, there is rarely any guidance as to how to answer the questions on them.

The Questions and Analysis series is therefore based on the belief that another approach should be added to those which already exist. It has two main aims.

The first is to separate narrative from interpretation so that the latter is no longer diluted by the former. Most chapters start with a background narrative section containing essential information. This material is then used in a section focusing on analysis through a specific question. The main purpose of this is to help to tighten up essay technique.

The second aim is to provide a comprehensive range of sources for each of the issues covered. The questions are of the type which appear on examination papers, and some have worked answers to demonstrate the techniques required.

The chapters may be approached in different ways. The background narratives can be read first to provide an overall perspective, followed by the analyses and then the sources. The alternative method is to work through all the components of each chapter before going on to the next.

ACKNOWLEDGEMENTS

The author and publishers would like to thank the following for permission to reproduce material from papers in their care or possession:

The Marquess of Salisbury for extracts from the papers of the third Marquess of Salisbury; the Public Record Office for extracts from cabinet and Foreign Office papers (Crown copyright); the National Trust (copyright owner) for the Hughenden papers; the National Library of Wales for the Earl Lloyd George papers; the Warden and Fellows of New College, Oxford, for the Viscount Milner papers; the Hon. Mrs Crispin Gascoigne for a quotation from Sir William Harcourt, in the W.E. Gladstone papers at the British Library; the Hon. Leo Amery for a quotation from L.S. Amery, in the Earl Lloyd George papers at the House of Lords Record Office; the National Archives of South Africa for the J.C. Smuts papers. The extract from a speech by Winston Churchill is reproduced with permission of Curtis Brown Ltd, London, on behalf of the estate of Sir Winston S. Churchill (copyright Winston S. Churchill). Author and publishers are also grateful to HarperCollins Publishers Ltd for permission to quote from J.A. Hobson, *Imperialism: A Study* and to Peters, Fraser and Dunlop for permission to quote from Hilaire Belloc, *The Modern Traveller*.

While every effort has been made to trace and acknowledge ownership of copyright material used in this volume, the publishers will be glad to make suitable arrangements with any copyright holders whom it has not been possible to contact.

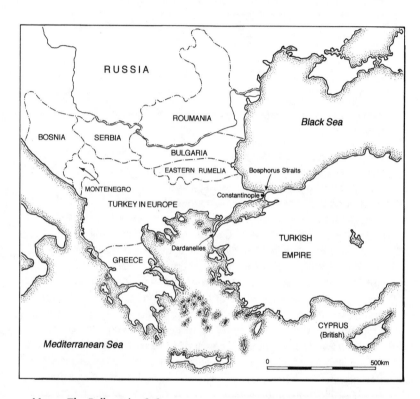

RUSSIA

ROUMANIA

Black Sea

BOSNIA

SERBIA

BULGARIA

EASTERN RUMELIA

Bosphorus Straits

MONTENEGRO

Constantinople

TURKEY IN EUROPE

TURKISH

Dardanelles

EMPIRE

GREECE

CYPRUS
(British)

Mediterranean Sea

0   500km

Map 1 The Balkans in 1878

1

THE PATRIOTIC PARTY
Disraeli, the Conservatives and Britain's world role

BACKGROUND NARRATIVE

In the decade and a half following the death of Lord Palmerston in 1865, British politics revolved around the rivalry of Benjamin Disraeli and William Ewart Gladstone, the leaders of the Conservative and Liberal parties respectively. These two statesmen competed for power in a country that stood at the peak of its power and influence. Britain's mid-Victorian economic position as the world's first industrial power was not yet seriously challenged by the rise of foreign competition. London stood at the centre of the international financial system and would continue to do so until the First World War. Naval supremacy underpinned Britain's leadership of a far-flung empire and enabled it to protect the world-wide commerce upon which its prosperity depended. Although the ending of the American Civil War in 1865 made possible the United States' emergence as the dominant power in the western hemisphere, it did not present an immediate threat to British interests. On the European continent, the most significant development of the period was the creation, through a series of wars, of a united Germany.

Disraeli spoke in 1870 of 'the German revolution, a greater political event than the French revolution of the last century'.[1] This was, however, the statement of an opposition leader, concerned to show up the inaction of the Gladstone government. In power after 1874, Disraeli initiated no major policy change in reaction to the unification of Germany. The defeat of France, Britain's traditional rival, by Germany in the war of 1870–1 was hardly a matter of great regret. Moreover under the cautious leadership of Otto von Bismarck, German Chancellor until 1890, the policy of the new Reich was largely directed towards the avoidance of further continental upheavals.

Nonetheless, British policy makers in the era of Disraeli and Gladstone were conscious that they lived in a changing world. At home, the first steps towards the democratisation of politics were taken with the passage of the 1867 Reform Act. The enfranchisement of large numbers of working men, followed shortly by measures to combat electoral intimidation and corruption, compelled political parties to organise themselves in a more modern and professional manner. In the 1860s the repeal of restrictive taxes on paper facilitated the rise of the popular press, while the 1870 Elementary Education Act initiated a significant growth in working-class literacy, with long-term implications for the character of the electorate. These developments meant that politicians of both parties increasingly had to shape their policies with the opinions and prejudices of a mass electorate in mind. Politics could no longer be viewed as the special preserve of an aristocratic elite, insulated from the feelings of the populace at large.

As they looked at the world outside, policy makers were aware of the weaknesses as well as the strengths of their country's position. Lacking a large standing army, active intervention in European affairs was not a realistic option for Britain. Disraeli's description of his country as adopting a stance of 'proud reserve' towards the continent was a reflection of this lack of military power. In any case British economic prosperity was tied closely to the maintenance of free trade and international peace. A major war would interrupt trade and necessitate increased domestic taxation, with unwelcome economic and political consequences in a nation accustomed to limited government intervention. Moreover, the very scale of Britain's empire could be viewed as a source of danger. A country with scattered imperial possessions and extensive trading interests was intensely vulnerable to pressure exerted by foreign rivals.

In the second half of the nineteenth century, as in the first, Britain continued to perceive France and Russia as its most likely foes. The need to resist expansion by the latter in the Near East, where it might conceivably threaten the routes to India, lynchpin of Britain's imperial system, involved successive governments in a particularly heavy commitment. Although it was increasingly decadent and corrupt, the maintenance of the Ottoman Empire was traditionally seen as the most effective barrier to Russia's desire for influence in the Balkans, leading to access to the Mediterranean. Britain had fought the Crimean War of 1854–6 to uphold the regime of the Turkish Sultan, widely regarded as 'the sick man of Europe', against the ambitions of Tsarist Russia. The Treaty of Paris, which closed the war, had guaranteed the Ottoman Empire's independence and had excluded Russian warships from the strategically important Black Sea. The growth of national sentiment among the Sultan's Christian subjects in the Balkans, exacerbated by Turkey's refusal to reform its inefficient and oppressive administrative system, introduced a dangerous element of instability to the region. The 'Eastern Question', with its ramifications for Britain's imperial power, was not the least of the problems faced by the governments of Victorian Britain.

ANALYSIS (1): HOW SUCCESSFUL WERE DISRAELI'S FOREIGN AND IMPERIAL POLICIES?

Of all the leading politicians of Queen Victoria's reign, Benjamin Disraeli remains perhaps the most controversial. He held the premiership only twice, for ten months in 1868 and then from 1874–80, and real power came to him relatively late in life. With his Jewish ancestry and his early reputation as a playboy and novelist, he lacked the traditional landed background and public school education shared by most of his fellow Conservatives. He had risen from the backbenches through his skills as a parliamentary debater and sustained himself against the prejudices of his own side through sheer force of personality. In the three short-lived Conservative governments of 1852, 1858–9 and 1866–8, he served as the indispensable lieutenant of the Prime Minister, the fourteenth Earl of Derby. The last of these governments undertook an action that has sometimes been seen as initiating a new period of British imperial expansion, the Abyssinian War of 1867–8. The arrest of some British officials by King Theodore of Abyssinia (present-day Ethiopia) was followed by the despatch of a military expedition by the Derby–Disraeli administration. The success of the expedition enabled Disraeli to associate the Conservative government with the vigorous defence of British overseas interests.

This theme was developed further by Disraeli in two celebrated speeches, at the Manchester Free Trade Hall and the Crystal Palace, delivered while the Conservatives were in opposition in 1872. In these speeches, and on other occasions, Disraeli highlighted the failure of Gladstone's Liberal government to uphold British prestige with sufficient determination. The Liberals had accepted the action taken by Russia two years earlier, when it had unilaterally repudiated the Black Sea clauses of the Treaty of Paris. More recently they had tamely paid compensation to the United States for damages caused by a British-built ship, the *Alabama*, during the American Civil War. Such concessions, according to Disraeli, would not have been granted by a Conservative Party committed to the maintenance of British imperial interests.

The electoral victory of February 1874 offered Disraeli an opportunity to give practical expression to his professed concern for the defence of the empire. Several steps towards the consolidation of British power in the tropics were taken in the first year of the government. In West Africa a new authority, the Gold Coast Protectorate, was created. British residents were installed in three of the Malay states, while in the southern Pacific, Fiji was annexed to the empire. In 1875 Disraeli engineered one of the most dramatic coups of his career when he purchased for Britain shares in the Suez Canal Company. These shares had belonged to the Khedive of Egypt, who administered the country on behalf of the Ottoman Empire and who by 1875 was financially overstretched. Disraeli took advantage of his difficulties to acquire a major stake in the canal, a waterway which provided a vital short-cut to Britain's Indian interests. The purchase enhanced British prestige and prevented the French, who had constructed the canal and were major shareholders in it, from exercising untrammelled influence in the region. It paved the way for a system of Anglo-French dual financial control over Egypt, which prevailed until the British occupation of the country in 1882.

The desire to consolidate British control over India had a bearing on another action of Disraeli's government, the passage of the Royal Titles Act in 1876. By declaring Queen Victoria Empress of India, the Act made her the equal of the Emperors of Russia, Germany and Austria-Hungary. It was also intended to increase the legitimacy of British rule in the eyes of the Indian princes and people. In fact the idea did not originate with Disraeli, and the timing of the Act was the outcome of pressure from the Queen herself. However, the publicity surrounding her elevation bore the characteristic stamp of a grand Disraelian gesture.

The central years of Disraeli's second ministry were dominated by a revival of the Eastern Question. At the end of 1875 the Ottoman Empire faced uprisings in two of its Balkan provinces, Bosnia and Herzegovina. Disraeli's response was conditioned by his distrust of Russian ambitions in the region and his concern to see Britain act as an independent, front-ranking power. Thus, when Germany, Russia and Austria issued the 'Berlin Memorandum' in May 1876, calling upon Turkey to introduce reforms in the discontented provinces, Disraeli refused to associate Britain with the document. Later that year his identification with the Ottoman Empire became a source of political embarrassment, when news reached Britain of savage Turkish repression following an uprising in Bulgaria. A massive popular agitation on behalf of the oppressed Bulgarian Christians, exploited by Gladstone and the Liberals, threatened to leave Disraeli dangerously isolated. His support for the Ottoman regime as a buffer against Russian expansionism seemed indefensible to an outraged public. Within the cabinet the Prime Minister's belligerently anti-Russian stance provoked a damaging confrontation with the pacific Foreign Secretary, the fifteenth Earl of Derby. Fortunately for Disraeli, now ensconced in the House of Lords as the Earl of Beaconsfield, opinion swung back in favour of his 'patriotic' stance when Russia attacked Turkey in April 1877. The government's decision to order the fleet to Constantinople, as a deterrent to further Russian aggression, attracted widespread popular support. There was little support for Derby, whose insistence on strict non-intervention drove him to resign from the government. By early 1878 humanitarian concern for the victims of Ottoman cruelty had been smothered by a wave of popular nationalism, or 'jingoism', a word derived from a popular music-hall verse of the day: 'we don't want to fight, but by jingo, if we do, we've got the ships, we've got the men, we've got the money too'.

In fact Disraeli achieved his aims without the need for military involvement. When the Russians imposed the punitive Treaty of San Stefano on a defeated Ottoman Empire in March 1878, they found Britain, Austria and Germany united against them in determination to secure a more equable settlement. The outcome was the Congress of Berlin, which Disraeli attended together with his new Foreign Secretary, Lord Salisbury. Russia was compelled to relinquish some of the gains made at San Stefano. In return for guaranteeing Turkish possessions in Asia, Britain acquired from the Sultan the island of Cyprus, a new base from which to protect the lines of communication to India. Disraeli enjoyed his greatest triumph when he returned to London in August 1878, claiming to have secured 'peace with honour' at Berlin.

In other aspects of external policy the Disraeli government enjoyed less resounding success. In Southern Africa the British colonies of Natal and Cape Colony co-existed uneasily with several independent black African kingdoms and two provinces established by Dutch (or Boer) settlers, the Transvaal and the Orange Free State. In an attempt to bring stability to a strategically important part of the African continent, Lord Carnarvon, Disraeli's Colonial Secretary, tried to bring about a federation of the British and Boer settlements. In 1877 he used the Boers' vulnerability to attack from the armies of the Zulu kingdom as a lever to secure the annexation of the Transvaal. Two years later the British High Commissioner in South Africa, Sir Bartle Frere, provoked a war with the Zulus in order to protect the Transvaal. To some extent this initiative can be excused by the need for rapid reactions by 'men on the spot' in an age of relatively slow communications over long distances. The war went badly for the British forces, which sustained a heavy defeat at Isandhlwana in January 1879. The Zulus were eventually defeated at considerable cost in terms of lives and money, with adverse consequences for the reputation of the imperial government.

Disraeli's South African difficulties coincided with the adoption of an equally contentious 'forward' policy on the north-west frontier of India. The Viceroy, Lord Lytton, was convinced that British control of the buffer state of Afghanistan was essential if Russian designs on the subcontinent were to be thwarted. Acting on his own initiative, Lytton sent British troops into Afghanistan at the end of 1878. The war initially went in Britain's favour and the Amir of Afghanistan was forced to accept the presence of a British military mission in his capital, Kabul. The following September, however, the mission was massacred, necessitating a renewal of hostilities. The situation was unresolved in the spring of 1880, when the Conservatives faced a general election in Britain. Their association with mismanaged conflicts on the frontiers of empire provided the Liberal opposition with effective ammunition in the electoral contest. In the celebrated Midlothian campaigns of 1879–80, Gladstone was able to depict the Disraeli government as authorising unnecessary, extravagant and immoral adventures, motivated by the empty pursuit of prestige. Although not the only factor in the heavy defeat suffered by Disraeli, the charge of imperial arrogance and incompetence undoubtedly played a part in his government's overthrow. It was an ironic outcome for a political leader who had so closely identified himself with the positive and effective defence of British overseas interests.

Questions

1. How effective was Disraeli's handling of the Eastern Question?
2. Have Disraeli's achievements in imperial affairs been exaggerated?

ANALYSIS (2): DID DISRAELI PUT INTO PRACTICE A COHERENT VISION OF BRITISH IMPERIAL INTERESTS IN HIS YEARS OF POWER?

Both critics and admirers of Disraeli traditionally credited him with a distinctive and consistent approach to the question of empire. To his political opponents, his association with a series of imperial adventures in the second half of the 1870s was thoroughly reprehensible. Following the Conservative leader's elevation to the House of Lords, Gladstone coined the term 'Beaconsfieldism' to describe the ideology that allegedly underpinned his rival's policies in the Near East, the Indian subcontinent and Southern Africa. From a more favourable standpoint, the 'official' biography, begun by W.F. Monypenny and completed by G.E. Buckle in the second decade of the twentieth century, portrayed its subject as the author of a far-sighted philosophy of imperial development. Thus the 1872 Crystal Palace speech is hailed as containing 'the famous declaration from which the modern conception of the British Empire largely takes its rise'.[2]

To many commentators, Disraeli's period of power was a preparation for the late nineteenth-century phenomenon known as 'the new imperialism'. In the decade after his death in 1881, the so-called 'scramble for Africa'[3] awakened a conscious spirit of militant expansionism in Britain. Disraeli's frequently expressed pride in Britain's overseas role, his unashamed emphasis on the pursuit of power and prestige, led many to see him as the architect of a new direction in external affairs. In more recent times the view of Disraeli as progenitor of a 'new imperialism' has enjoyed a revival in the work of the historian Freda Harcourt. Focusing on the Derby–Disraeli government of 1866–8, Harcourt argues that these years witnessed a deliberate stimulation of popular imperial sentiment by a government beset with domestic problems. The Abyssinian expedition of 1867 was conceived as a way of drawing public attention away from economic hardship and of smothering unrest over the issue of parliamentary reform. According to this argument, the expedition's success vindicated Disraeli's belief that all classes could be united behind a truly national policy.[4]

Such interpretations have not, however, commanded universal support among historians. A close examination of the origins of the 1867 war has shown that the crisis was driven more by events in Abyssinia than by a conscious policy initiated by the British government.[5] The correspondence of leading ministers betrays a sense of anxiety about the practical difficulties of mounting the expedition. There is little hard evidence to connect Disraeli himself with its planning. Moreover, it is worth pointing out that the primary purpose of the war was to rescue British captives and to inflict a signal punishment on the Abyssinian ruler for his defiance of British power. After achieving these goals, the troops were withdrawn without any attempt to annex the country for the empire. This contrasts sharply with the more overtly expansionist concerns of policy makers during the later 'scramble for Africa'.

Such considerations lend support to those historians who see Disraeli not as the author of a new imperial ideology, but as an opportunist whose interest in the empire was shallow. Cynical interpretations of the Conservative leader's career argue that, although hitherto indifferent to 'imperialism', he adopted the issue in the 1870s for its value as an electoral weapon. Much has been made of quotations from two of Disraeli's letters to colleagues, in which he expressed exasperation with the self-governing colonies in North America. In 1852 he wrote that 'these wretched colonies will all be independent, too, in a few years, and are a millstone round our necks'. Fourteen years later we find him asking 'what is the use of these colonial deadweights which we do not govern?'[6] We should, however, beware of reliance on quotations lifted out of context. On both occasions Disraeli, as Chancellor of the Exchequer, was reacting to the unwillingness of certain British North American colonies to take financial responsibility for their own defence. These remarks tell us nothing about his attitude towards other imperial possessions. Even in the particular cases to which they relate, there can be no grounds for claiming that Disraeli wished to see a weakening of ties with the mother country.

Nonetheless, it would be naïve to attempt to divorce Disraeli's pronouncements on empire from their political context. In an important study Richard Koebner and Helmut Schmidt established that the timing of the 1872 Crystal Palace speech was determined by Disraeli's need to reassert his leadership of the Conservative Party in the face of an internal challenge.[7] The section of the speech which dealt with imperial issues focused on the omissions of Liberal governments, rather than on Conservative plans for the future. Although Disraeli expressed regret that arrangements had not been made for colonial tariff and defence policies, and that the cause of imperial federation had been neglected, this did not constitute a statement of intent.

What, then, was the nature of Disraeli's contribution to the empire in his years of power? He manifested little practical interest in the self-governing colonies and was not an enthusiast for the territorial expansion of the empire. In part this was the consequence of personal factors. By 1874 he was almost seventy; his health was poor and his grasp of policy detail was imperfect. The advice of his private secretary, Montagu Corry, who reported to the Prime Minister on public reaction to government policies, carried a great deal of weight with him. Disraeli's attitude to his ministerial colleagues was typified by his words to Lord Carnarvon, his Colonial Secretary, on the subject of South Africa: 'In all these affairs I must trust to you . . . Do what you think wisest.'[8] Moreover, as W.D. McIntyre has demonstrated in the cases of West Africa, Malaya and Fiji, the parameters of government policy were often set by decisions taken by Lord Kimberley, Colonial Secretary in the first Gladstone administration, and his colleagues: 'far from Disraeli initiating a "forward movement" in 1874, his Government merely went ahead with policies worked out by their Liberal predecessors'.[9]

Although capable of seizing the limelight at certain critical moments, Disraeli was happy to delegate to others where possible. The difficulties that he faced were due in part to a failure to retain adequate oversight of enthusiastic subordinates. Disraeli was in the unfortunate position of publicly defending actions taken by 'men on the spot' without his prior consent. Referring in his Guildhall speech of November 1878 to Lord Lytton's forward policy in Afghanistan, he spoke of the problem of India's north-west boundary, which he described as 'a haphazard, not a scientific frontier'. Privately, however, Disraeli wrote that 'when V-Roys [viceroys] and Comms.[commanders]-in-chief disobey orders, they ought to be sure of success in their mutiny'.[10] The difficulties of exercising effective control over officials at a distance, before the era of instant communication, help to explain the position in which Disraeli found himself. Yet he cannot be acquitted of all responsibility. It is at least arguable that, by his rhetoric, he helped to create a climate in which men like Lytton were encouraged to adopt an aggressive approach.

Disraeli did not, then, bring to office a far-reaching scheme of imperial expansion and consolidation. Much of what occurred under his two premierships consisted of pragmatic, unplanned responses to events. The work of Marvin Swartz, among others, has highlighted the way in which domestic political pressures helped to shape Disraeli's policies. The decision to purchase shares in the Suez Canal Company, for example, may be partly explained by the fact that, by late 1875, the Conservatives' domestic agenda had been largely fulfilled. It was also the kind of grand gesture that served to distract attention from a series of embarrassments involving the current First Lord of the Admiralty.[11] Yet it would misrepresent Disraeli to suggest that he was always driven by domestic factors. Had this been the case, in 1876 he would surely have reversed his pro-Turkish policy when it proved unpopular at the time of the Bulgarian massacres.

In many ways Disraeli's vision of empire recalled that of Gladstone's predecessor as Liberal leader, Lord Palmerston. In the 1850s and early 1860s the latter had enjoyed tremendous popularity through his unashamed and often flamboyant defence of British interests. It was no accident that, within a few months of taking office in 1874, Disraeli wrote to a confidant that 'I believe since Palmerston we have never been so energetic, and in a year's time we shall be more.'[12] Like his role model, Disraeli laid constant stress on the importance of upholding British prestige and prosperity. At the height of the Eastern crisis, in May 1876, he bluntly informed the Queen that 'Your Majesty's fleet has not been ordered to the Mediterranean to protect Christians or Turks, but to uphold Your Majesty's Empire.'[13] When Disraeli thought of the British Empire, he thought primarily of India, with its great wealth and unique strategic importance. This explains his emphasis on the importance of protecting the sea routes to the East. In 1863 he told the House of Commons that Britain 'has been constantly congratulated on having a chain of Mediterranean garrisons, which secured our Indian Empire'.[14] He differed from the next generation of politicians in attaching little strategic importance to Africa. Instead he subscribed to the older idea, that the security of India depended on resisting Russian designs upon Constantinople and the Straits of Constantinople. He stated emphatically that 'if the Russians had Constantinople, they could at any time march their army through Syria to the mouth of the Nile . . . Constantinople is the key of India, not Egypt and the Suez Canal.'[15]

Disraeli's close involvement with the Eastern Question during his second government stemmed from his belief that the region was vital to the maintenance of British power in the world. The role of the empire was to buttress Britain's international position and to enable it to act as a great power. In the words of S.R. Stembridge, 'his imperial ideal was a powerful England, strengthened by the resources and peoples of a far-flung empire, playing a decisive role in world affairs'.[16]

In the second half of the 1870s this perception of Britain's overseas role meshed neatly with the political self-interest of the Conservative Party. Disraeli was able to present his party as the natural representatives of the healthy patriotic instincts of the British people, who were 'proud of belonging to a great country, and wish to maintain its greatness . . . they are proud of belonging to an Imperial country, and are resolved to maintain, if they can, their empire'.[17] By contrast the Gladstonian Liberals, with their moralistic reservations about the use of national power, could plausibly be portrayed as culpably weak in their defence of British interests. As Robert Blake argues, the ability to attach the label of 'spiritual treason' to their political opponents was to be a powerful weapon in the Conservative Party's political armoury during the next century.[18]

It is not necessary to depict Disraeli as the prophet of a 'new imperialism' in order to give him credit for a serious commitment to the British Empire. His view of his country's world role was an essentially traditionalist one. He came to power with a determination to assert what he regarded as Britain's 'just position' in Europe and in the wider world. This did not necessarily entail the annexation of further territory, but it did require a determined defence of existing positions. In that, at least, he remained consistent throughout his career.

Questions

1. How far was Disraeli's imperial policy determined by domestic factors?
2. How forward-looking was Disraeli's concept of the British Empire?

SOURCES

DISRAELI'S FOREIGN AND IMPERIAL POLICIES, 1874–80

Source A: from Disraeli's speech at the Crystal Palace, 24 June 1872.

If you look to the history of this country since the advent of Liberalism – forty years ago – you will find that there has been no effort so continuous, so subtle, supported by so much energy, and carried on with so much ability and acumen, as the attempts of Liberalism to effect the disintegration of the Empire of England . . . It has been proved to all of us that we have lost money by our Colonies. It has been shown with precise, with mathematical demonstration, that there never was a jewel in the Crown of England that was so truly costly as the possession of India.

Source B: Disraeli defends his Egyptian policy in the House of Commons, 8 February 1876.

Some may take an economical view of the subject, some may take a commercial view, some may take a peaceful view, some may take a warlike view of it; but of this I feel persuaded – and I speak with confidence – that when I appeal to the House of Commons for their vote they will agree with the country, that this was a purchase which was necessary to maintain the Empire, and which favours in every degree the policy which this country ought to sustain.

Source C: Disraeli's private secretary, Montagu Corry, reports to his master on the Conservative victory in the Salford by-election, 19 April 1877.

I find the House fully alive to the importance of the Salford victory: – our men elate [i.e. are elated] – almost dismay in the camp of the enemy! I have taken some pains to ascertain the 'raison' of the result, and have data for a decided opinion that the election turned on the Foreign question mainly . . . the feeling of the working class is neither for Russia, nor for Turkey, but thoroughly excited at the prospect of the interests or honour of England being touched.

I sounded both [Conservative speakers at the by-election] as to whether they, or anyone else, had touched on this point and its future aspect *in its details* – the freedom of the Straits, or otherwise. 'Not at all,' they say, 'the subject is not within the present comprehension of the working classes.['] It is evident that, in *particulars*, some education will be needed; in *general*, I feel assured that Lancashire is determined that England shall not kiss the feet of Russia.

Source D: the Foreign Secretary, Lord Derby, writes to Lord Salisbury, 23 December 1877.

I know our chief of old, and . . . I am fully convinced – not indeed that he wants a war – but that he has made up his mind to large military preparations, to an extremely warlike speech, to an agitation in favour of armed intervention (recollect that he said in Cabinet: 'The country is asleep and I want to wake it up'), and if possible to an expedition that shall occupy Constantinople or Gallipoli . . . He believes thoroughly in 'prestige' as all foreigners do, and would think it (quite sincerely) in the interests of the country to spend 200 millions on a war if the result was to make foreign States think more highly of us as a military power. These ideas are intelligible but they are not mine nor yours and their being sincerely held does not make them less dangerous.

Questions

*1. Explain the reference in Source B to 'a purchase which was necessary to maintain the Empire'. [2]

2. In what respects are Sources A and B similar in terms of purpose and content? [5]

3. Using your own knowledge of the events of 1876–7, explain the context of the reference in Source C: 'England shall not kiss the feet of Russia'. [5]

4. In view of the authorship, language and tone of Sources C and D, how reliable would you expect these documents to be as evidence for the study of Disraeli's actions in this period? [6]

5. Using your knowledge of the period, how complete a picture do these sources give of Disraeli's attitudes towards the conduct of Britain's external policies? [7]

Worked answer

*1. [This question requires a short but precise answer. Notice that only two marks are allocated to it.]

The reference is to Disraeli's purchase in 1875 of the Khedive's shares in the Suez Canal Company. The canal's usefulness as a route to India explains his claim that the purchase was important for the British Empire.

2

LATE VICTORIAN LIBERALISM AND EMPIRE
The era of Gladstone

BACKGROUND NARRATIVE

William Ewart Gladstone was the most prominent political figure of the second half of Queen Victoria's reign. This was due in part to the sheer length of his official career. Having first entered government as a Conservative under Sir Robert Peel in the 1830s, by 1859 he had completed his transition to Liberalism. Ten years later he was the acknowledged leader of the Liberal Party, a position he retained for the next two and a half decades. After serving a thorough apprenticeship as Chancellor of the Exchequer, he went on to hold the premiership for an unparalleled four terms, from 1868–74, 1880–5, February to July 1886 and 1892–4.

It was impossible for Gladstone's politically conscious contemporaries to be indifferent to him. To his followers in the country, he was the revered embodiment of a moral approach to politics, a man whose public life was rooted in a deep Christian faith. Gladstone's opponents, however, viewed him as a self-righteous humbug, masking selfish calculation behind professions of high principle. All sections of opinion concurred, however, in acknowledging his skills as a parliamentarian and a communicator. Gladstone's public profile evolved through his command of platform oratory, his authorship of numerous pamphlets and exploitation of the popular press. He became one of the first front-ranking politicians to develop a successful relationship with a mass audience.

Another source of Gladstone's long political dominance was his unique ability to reconcile the various factions composing the Victorian Liberal Party. According to one of its leading members, Sir William Harcourt, 'like the Kingdom of Heaven, the Liberal Party is a house of many mansions'.[1] Socially, it was headed by aristocratic Whigs, the inheritors of long family traditions of executive leadership. The party also drew substantial support from the commercial and industrial middle classes, many of whom held radical political views derived from membership of the nonconformist Churches. These men dominated the party organisation at local level and provided a growing number of Liberal MPs. Beyond them, the party attracted the allegiance of upwardly mobile working men, artisans and shopkeepers imbued with the Liberal ethos of liberty, self-improvement and social progress. At least until 1886, when Gladstone's adoption of Irish Home Rule split his party, he managed to maintain a framework within which these groups, with their varied and often contradictory views, could co-exist.

Strains within this coalition were particularly evident in the field of foreign and imperial affairs. Together with much of the party's broad centre, the Whigs subscribed to a traditional view of diplomacy, based upon a robust defence of Britain's interests. More idealistic Liberals wanted to see Britain exercise moral leadership within Europe, promoting the right of small nations to self-determination. At odds with both groups were radicals like Richard Cobden and John Bright, leaders of the near-pacifist, non-interventionist 'Manchester school'. With their faith in the capacity of free trade to reconcile the peoples of the world, the Cobdenites renounced 'secret diplomacy' and 'militarism' as the tools of self-interested aristocratic elites. They opposed intervention in other states' affairs, not only because they regarded it as unjust, but as it imposed additional tax burdens. It should be noted that, by the criteria of nineteenth-century Liberalism, increases in taxation were themselves viewed as inherently immoral.

ANALYSIS (1): HOW EFFECTIVE WAS GLADSTONE'S MANAGEMENT OF EXTERNAL CRISES?

As Gladstone told his last Foreign Secretary, Lord Rosebery, he regarded co-operation between the holder of that office and the Prime

Minister as the crucial relationship in foreign policy making.[2] In his first administration the Foreign Office was occupied by two Whigs in succession: Lord Clarendon, who died in June 1870, and Lord Granville, a personal friend of the Prime Minister. The transition coincided with the onset of the first serious external crisis faced by the ministry, the Franco-Prussian War. Britain played no direct part in the war beyond securing from both participants a commitment to respect Belgium's neutrality. The cabinet made no protest against Bismarck's annexation of the French provinces of Alsace and Lorraine. Nor was Britain able to take effective action when, in October 1870, Russia took advantage of the crisis to repudiate the Black Sea clauses of the 1856 Treaty of Paris. The most that Gladstone could do was to host a great power conference which gave the gloss of international approval to Russia's unilateral action.

The other significant event of the first government was Gladstone's acceptance, in 1872, of international arbitration in the *Alabama* case. The damage done to Northern shipping by this British-built vessel during the American Civil War had been a running sore in relations with the United States. When the verdict of the tribunal in Geneva went against Britain and damages of £3.25 million were awarded, Gladstone incurred considerable unpopularity by accepting the ruling. The episode illustrated his commitment to substituting the collective verdict of international opinion for the conflicts of rival nations. He stated that the amount of compensation was 'dust in the balance compared with the moral value of the example set'.[3]

In opposition after the election defeat of 1874, Gladstone placed foreign and imperial affairs at the heart of his attacks on Disraeli's government. The Conservative leader's apparent indifference to the Ottoman Empire's oppression of its Bulgarian subjects provided Gladstone with an ideal moral platform. His call for the Turks, 'one and all, bag and baggage', to 'clear out from the province they have desolated and profaned' placed him at the head of a powerful popular movement of opinion.[4] In the months prior to the general election of 1880, the Bulgarian atrocities agitation broadened into a general attack on Conservative overseas policies. The thrust of Gladstone's two Midlothian campaigns was that Disraeli had involved the country in immoral, costly and unnecessary adventures. In place of the Disraelian pursuit of prestige and power Gladstone offered six principles for the conduct of foreign policy. It should be based upon 'just legislation and economy at home' and should seek to preserve 'the blessings of peace'. Selfish national aims should be restrained by working with other powers in 'what is called the Concert of Europe'. Britain should 'avoid needless and entangling engagements' and should 'acknowledge the equal rights of all nations'. Finally, 'the foreign policy of England should always be inspired by the love of freedom'.[5]

Gladstone's return to power with a clear majority gave him the opportunity to demonstrate how far these ideals were compatible with external realities. Lord Granville, who shared Gladstone's broad approach to foreign affairs, was reappointed Foreign Secretary. Initially, Gladstone's conception of a European concert, acting in defence of international law, enjoyed some success. In 1880 he organised an allied naval demonstration in the Adriatic, with the intention of compelling the Turks to honour prior commitments to transfer land to Montenegro and Greece. He also managed to extricate Britain from Afghanistan, where the previous government had left British interests in a precarious position. The Liberals negotiated a settlement that gave Britain control of the Khyber Pass and other strategically important points, while leaving Afghanistan as an independent buffer state between British India and Russia.

In general, however, Gladstone found it more difficult to liquidate the entanglements that he inherited from his predecessor. Although Gladstone had condemned Disraeli's acquisition of Cyprus and wished to cede it to Greece, he was unable to do so. After his diatribes against Ottoman cruelty he could scarcely expect Sultan Abdul Hamid, the island's legal sovereign, to give his consent. More serious difficulties arose in South Africa where Gladstone failed to withdraw as quickly as the Boer population wished. Although Gladstone was prepared to reverse the Conservatives' annexation of the Transvaal, he failed to communicate this before its President, Paul Kruger, led his people in rebellion at the end of 1880. Their subsequent annihilation of a British force at Majuba Hill in February 1881 earned Gladstone the contempt of a large section of domestic opinion. The eventual outcome, the Convention of Pretoria, represented a belated victory for Gladstonian ideas of national self-determination, at least in relation to the white settler community. The Boer republics were granted their independence, subject to British 'suzerainty', a general control over their external relations.

It was in Egypt that Gladstone's ideals faced their most severe test. In September 1881, a nationalist revolt broke out under the leadership of Colonel Arabi, an Egyptian army officer. The rebellion was a challenge not only to the Khedive, the nominal ruler of Egypt, but also to the control exercised jointly by Britain and France over the country's financial affairs. In line with his Midlothian principles, and distracted by a resurgence of trouble in Ireland, Gladstone was at first reluctant to intervene. If action had to be taken, he insisted that it must be with the approval of other European powers. In the event he allowed himself to be persuaded of the need for unilateral British action. Anti-European rioting in June 1882 was followed by a British naval bombardment and the despatch of a military expedition. Gladstone defended the move on the grounds that the safety of the Suez Canal Zone was threatened by incipient anarchy in Egypt. One cabinet minister, John Bright, resigned in protest at his colleagues' resort to the use of force. In September, the French having withdrawn their support, the British Army decisively defeated Arabi at Tel el Kebir and installed a Consul-General to 'advise' the Khedive. Although Gladstone maintained that Britain would withdraw as soon as possible, his action led in practice to an occupation which lasted until the middle of the twentieth century.

The invasion indirectly involved Gladstone in a further embarrassment. The Egyptian government traditionally laid claim to the neighbouring territory of the Sudan. In 1883 its authority was successfully challenged by a nationalist revolt, led by a charismatic religious extremist known as the Mahdi. In spite of strong pressure to undertake the conquest of the Sudan, Gladstone refused to contemplate British involvement beyond Egypt's borders. Unfortunately, the soldier whom Gladstone sent to supervise the evacuation of Egyptian garrisons in the Sudan, General Charles Gordon, was an unwise choice. Following his own imperialist instincts, Gordon remained in the Sudanese capital, Khartoum, where he was surrounded by the Mahdi's forces. By the time that a reluctant Gladstone had decided to send a relief expedition it was too late to save the disobedient Gordon from massacre. The merits of Gladstone's case for limiting British commitments received little attention in the ensuing public uproar. In early 1885 he was widely charged with inadequate concern for British imperial interests and his popular title, the G.O.M. (Grand Old Man), was reversed to read M.O.G. (Murderer of Gordon).

Before the fall of his second government Gladstone recovered a little political credit in 1885 through his handling of a crisis with Russia. A long period of tension over the exact delineation of the Afghan border culminated in a confrontation at Penjdeh. Uncharacteristically, Gladstone mobilised troops, forcing the Tsarist regime to accept a compromise settlement. In the interests of obtaining a stable frontier with Russia the Liberal government had shown a willingness to risk war. It is not surprising that many historians have interpreted Gladstone's reaction to the crisis as a ploy to cover his retreat from the Sudanese fiasco.

In Gladstone's last two administrations, his personal involvement in foreign policy was much reduced. This was largely due to his absorption in his last great crusade for Irish Home Rule. In both 1886 and 1892 he chose as Foreign Secretary Lord Rosebery, one of the dwindling band of aristocratic Liberals who remained loyal to Gladstone after the split over Ireland. As the ageing leader of a party now seriously weakened, Gladstone needed Rosebery's membership of his cabinet. The latter's ideas proved uncongenial. Rosebery was a convinced 'Liberal imperialist', determined to maintain British involvement in Egypt and the surrounding region. In January 1893 he secured cabinet approval for the reinforcement of Britain's military presence in Egypt, overcoming the resistance of a Prime Minister who declared that he would as soon set fire to Westminster Abbey as give his consent.[6] Rosebery also secured the transformation of Uganda – viewed by the imperial-minded as strategically important for the defence of Egypt – into a British protectorate after a cabinet battle with Gladstone.

The issue on which Gladstone chose to resign in March 1894, his opposition to increased naval spending, was entirely appropriate. By standing out against his colleagues' readiness to engage in an arms build-up, Gladstone demonstrated his attachment to the values of mid-Victorian Liberalism. It was fitting that he should be succeeded as Prime Minister by Rosebery, who identified positively with the new spirit of imperial activity.

The circumstances of Gladstone's retirement underlined the difficulties of sustaining traditional Liberal ideals in a less favourable international environment. Gladstone's handling of the Egyptian and Penjdeh crises in his second administration demonstrated that, under pressure, he could emulate Disraeli in the use of force on the frontiers of empire. Nonetheless, his public identification with the rhetoric of the Midlothian campaign involved him in embarrassments, which a more coolly pragmatic approach might have avoided. Classic Gladstonian Liberalism was appropriate to a relatively brief period, when the European continent was tranquil and great power conflicts were muted. By the 1890s, with the development of rival alliance systems and the emergence of pressing imperial issues in Africa and elsewhere, its idealism seemed increasingly irrelevant.

Questions

1. 'The ministry of all the troubles.' With reference to imperial affairs, explain why this label has been attached to Gladstone's 1880–5 government.

2. Did Gladstone sacrifice national interests to abstract moral principles?

ANALYSIS (2): DID GLADSTONIAN LIBERALISM OFFER A DISTINCTIVE APPROACH TO FOREIGN AND IMPERIAL AFFAIRS?

Many older studies of Gladstone were shaped by the interpretative framework adopted by his friend, colleague and official biographer, John Morley. In his life of Gladstone, published in 1903, Morley presented his subject's career as a progression from reactionary Toryism to enlightened Liberalism. The underlying theme was Gladstone's steady awakening over a long period to the importance of freedom as a guide to political action. Thirty years later Paul Knaplund, the first historian to make a detailed study of Gladstone's foreign and imperial policy, characterised his ideas as 'faith in eternal verities, in the perfectibility of man and his institutions, in the ultimate victory of right over might, in the healthy qualities of freedom'. A range of domestic political pressures, together with numerous external commitments, restricted Gladstone's scope for applying his principles without detracting from the nobility of the attempt.[7]

Even before Gladstone finally joined the Liberal Party, he showed himself as having a great deal in common with the pacific, internationalist outlook of Cobdenism. He shared the radical belief that large expenditure on armaments was an unwarranted drain on taxpayers' resources as well as a dangerous encouragement to an aggressive foreign policy. His promotion of the Anglo-French free-trade treaty of 1860 reflected the classic Liberal belief that commercial links between nations would reduce political tensions. In his private and public pronouncements alike he displayed a remarkable lack of jealousy and suspicion with regard to the intentions of other powers. He declared himself ready to 'welcome the Germans as our neighbours in South Africa'[8] and dismissed as alarmist fears that the building of a Channel tunnel would endanger British security. 'Since the Norman Conquest,' he asserted, 'the English have invaded France at least ten times as often as the French have invaded England.'[9]

The tendency in recent Gladstone scholarship, however, has been to emphasise the enduring conservatism of many of his attitudes. Colin Matthew, the editor of Gladstone's diaries, shows how he approached international affairs from a different philosophical standpoint to that of the Manchester school. While acknowledging the way in which

Gladstone's free-trade views encouraged an anti-imperialist frame of mind, Matthew writes that on the other hand 'his executive itch, his sense of the immediate, of what seemed to be "practical", encouraged imperial action eventually as bold as that of any other Victorian'. Again, 'foreign policy was not, as it was for the Radicals, corrupt dealings between landed castes, but rather the means by which European nations communicated for the public good'.[10] Gladstone's belief in 'a European conscience expressed by the collective guarantee and concerted action of the European powers'[11] derived from his deeply felt High Anglican faith.

Gladstone's philosophy opened the way to involvement in continental affairs in a way quite alien to the strict non-interventionism of the Cobdenite outlook. Thus, as he declared during the Franco-Prussian War, England's 'hand will not be unready to be lifted up, on every fit and hopeful occasion, in sustaining the general sense of Europe against a disturber of the public peace'.[12] Although Britain's limited military resources ruled out intervention in a major continental war, Gladstone was no pacifist. In certain circumstances he was prepared to use force, or the threat of force, as was shown by the anti-Turkish naval demonstration of 1880 and the Penjdeh incident five years later. In private he resisted parallels between himself and his Crimean War predecessor, Lord Aberdeen, whose record in upholding British interests was much derided. In a letter to Granville in November 1870 Gladstone wrote that 'all know the mischief done by the Russian idea of Lord Aberdeen[,] and the Opposition are in the habit of studiously representing me as his double, or his heir, in pacific traditions. This I do not conceive to be true.'[13]

Gladstone's attitude to Britain's imperial power was also more complex than was once assumed. While there seems no reason to doubt his personal aversion to the expansion of overseas responsibilities, he accepted the existing limits of the British Empire. His first government completed the withdrawal of British troops from New Zealand, a policy initiated by earlier administrations, and took similar steps with regard to Canada. As C.C. Eldridge has shown, the aim was to make the self-governing colonies responsible for their own defence, while carrying out a cost-cutting reorganisation of Britain's troop deployments. Certainly there was no intention on Gladstone's part to break the link between Britain and its overseas settlements.[14]

A strong sense of order co-existed with Gladstone's belief in liberty. The work of C.F. Goodfellow and D.M. Schreuder, for example, has underlined the conservative dimension of Gladstone's South African policy. It seems that Gladstone's real intention towards the Transvaal in

1880–1 was not to concede self-determination pure and simple. His real preference was for a federalist strategy within which Boer aspirations and British strategic needs could be reconciled.[15] Nor, in spite of his much publicised indignation on behalf of the victims of Ottoman massacres in the Balkans, did he give unqualified support to the subject peoples of other empires. His objection was not to the fact of the Ottoman Empire but to the way in which the Turks had abused a position of power. He did not call for the ending of the Sultan's sovereignty but for united European action to bring about 'local liberty and practical self-government' in the particular provinces affected by oppression.

These examples illustrate the truth of Keith Sandiford's claim that the conservatism and complexity of Gladstone's mind have often been underestimated.[16] 'Gladstonian Liberalism' was not a static ideology but a set of values that evolved over time. The extent to which they influenced policy making depended on a changing balance of forces. Gladstone's cabinets were not packed with like-minded individuals but with representatives of the Whig, moderate and radical viewpoints. In his first government in particular the Prime Minister was highly successful in reconciling the various strands of opinion. For example, in the Black Sea clauses affair of 1870, Gladstone satisfied Whig feeling by his firmness in bringing Russia to the conference table. At the same time the manoeuvre reassured the Liberal left by avoiding the immorality and expense of military preparations.

Gladstone did not always prevail over his colleagues. A determined movement at cabinet level could thwart him as when Foreign Secretary Granville and others prevented him from protesting against Prussia's annexation of Alsace–Lorraine in September 1870. In Gladstone's second cabinet, fierce debates preceded the taking of decisions on South Africa, Egypt and the Sudan. The support of Lord Hartington[17] and most of the Whig ministers for firmness in defending imperial interests was predictable. Within the radical camp, matters were more complicated, with John Bright resigning over the bombardment of Alexandria in 1882 and Joseph Chamberlain supporting the intervention.

Public opinion, channelled through Parliament, the press and numerous pressure groups – commercial interests, missionary societies and other bodies – also had an influence on policy making. Although its impact is hard to measure precisely, it should not be discounted. It certainly played a part in preventing ministers from withdrawing from imperial commitments. Lord Kimberley, Colonial Secretary from 1870–4, was certainly not an instinctive expansionist, writing privately that 'when I begin to entertain projects of an African Empire . . . I hope that I shall be put at once in a strait waistcoat'. W.D. McIntyre's work on the extension of British control in the tropics demonstrates the role of Kimberley's junior colleague, Edward Knatchbull-Hugessen, in urging the political inexpediency of withdrawal.[18] Kimberley's Conservative successor, Lord Carnarvon, was told by J.T. Delane, editor of *The Times*, that withdrawal from the Gold Coast was not an option in an age of mass journalism. 'The world is growing so small that every patch of territory begins to be looked upon as a stray farm is by a County magnate. Besides, the British Public will not excuse you from the task of civilising the Ashantis.'[19]

While domestic pressures may have helped to push the Gladstone governments in unexpected directions, the actions of foreign powers frequently conspired to frustrate the Prime Minister's intentions. It was Gladstone's misfortune to co-exist with Bismarck, whose cynical pursuit of German interests left little room for the kind of European concert that the former favoured. In the 1880s Bismarck constructed a series of alliances in order to ensure the isolation of France and to maintain a balance of power between Austria and Russia in the Balkans. This helps to explain why Gladstone was unable to secure French collaboration for his Egyptian policy in 1882. His prospective partner feared that Bismarck's readiness to see French troops involved in the Middle East might be a diversionary tactic to cover a hostile German move in Europe. The fact that Egypt's financial arrangements depended on the approval of an international commission gave Bismarck further scope to make difficulties. The situation enabled him to follow a policy of polite blackmail designed to extort colonial concessions from the British. Thus, with Egypt facing the prospect of bankruptcy in early 1885, we find Gladstone urging Granville to press forward 'the settlement for the north coast of New Guinea . . . It is really impossible to exaggerate the importance of getting out of the way the bar to the Egyptian settlement.'[20]

By the end of his political career, Gladstone regarded himself as an outdated figure, 'a dead man, one fundamentally a Peel–Cobden man'. His stubborn opposition to the 'militarism' of the 1894 naval estimates represented an important thread of continuity with his earlier career. He was as reluctant to annex Uganda in 1893 as he had been to sanction increased commitments in the Gold Coast twenty years earlier. Yet executive responsibility frequently compelled him to adopt policies very different from the positions he had taken while in opposition. It was richly ironic that, in 1877, he had warned against establishing British rule in the Suez Canal Zone: 'our first site in Egypt, be it by larceny or be it by emption [purchase], will be the almost certain egg of a North African Empire'.[21] In 1882, facing a combination of domestic political pressures, strategic needs and economic considerations, he would himself fulfil that prophecy.

It is not enough, however, to argue that events alone prevented Gladstone from realising a consistent and distinctive vision of Britain's role in the world. That vision was in important respects deeply conservative. He assessed national liberation movements on their individual merits, handling Kruger, Arabi and the Mahdi in widely different ways. If he stressed the importance of 'the general judgement of civilised mankind', he gave little or no thought to the kind of institutions that might give it permanence. In essentials he accepted the traditional concert of Europe machinery, based upon the co-operation of aristocratic elites. It was left to his twentieth-century heirs to attempt to replace old-fashioned 'secret diplomacy' with a League of Nations. Although Gladstone anticipated the growth of a new and more democratic international order, he contributed little to its practical realisation.

Questions

1. In what ways did Gladstone's approach to foreign affairs differ from that of other Liberals?
2. Why did Gladstone fail to achieve his ideal of a 'concert of Europe'?

SOURCES

LIBERALISM AND EMPIRE, 1879–85

Source A: a report of Gladstone's speech at Dalkeith, 26 November 1879.

He insisted that we should ever 'remember the rights of the savage, as we call him.' 'Remember,' he exclaimed, 'that the sanctity of life in the hill villages of Afghanistan, among the winter snows, is as inviolable in the eye of Almighty God as can be your own. Remember that He who has united you as human beings in the same flesh and blood, has bound you by the law of mutual love, that that mutual love is not limited by the laws of this island, is not limited by the boundaries of Christian civilisation; that it passes over the whole surface of the earth, and embraces the meanest along with the greatest in its unmeasured scope.'

Source B: from Gladstone's speech at Edinburgh, 29 November 1879.

Whatever we may say amidst the clash of arms and amidst the din of preparation for warfare in time of peace – amidst all this yet there is going on a profound mysterious movement, that whether we will or not, is bringing the nations of the civilised world, as well as the uncivilised, morally as well as physically nearer to one another, and making them more and more responsible before God for one another's welfare.

Source C: a letter from Lord Granville, Gladstone's Foreign Secretary to an absent cabinet colleague, Lord Spencer, 22 June 1882.

We have had several Cabinets more or less formal about Egypt.
Bright, of course, the most peaceable. Chamberlain almost the greatest Jingo.
I am ready to go any lengths for reparation, and I set great store about making the Canal safe. But I own to dreadful alarm at occupying Egypt militarily and politically with the French. I think the majority would rather like to do this.
Gladstone does not like being in a hurry about the Suez Canal, but rather took us by surprise by proposing himself the big words in case the Turks refused to send troops. It is a nasty business, and we have been much out of luck.

Source D: from Gladstone's letter to John Bright, 14 July 1882.

The general situation in Egypt had latterly become one in which everything was governed by sheer military violence. Every legitimate authority – the Khedive, the Sultan, the notables ... had been put down, and a situation of *force* had been created, which could only be met by force. This being so, we had laboured to the uttermost, almost alone but not without success to secure that if force were employed against the violence of Arabi it should be force armed with the highest sanction of law: that it should be the force of the sovereign, authorised and restrained by the united Powers of Europe, who in such a case, represent the civilised world.

... [Our action in bombarding Alexandria] has taught many lessons, struck a heavy, perhaps a deadly blow at the reign of violence, brought again into light the beginnings of legitimate rule, shown the fanaticism of the East that massacre of Europeans is not likely to be perpetrated with impunity and greatly advanced the Egyptian question towards a permanent and peaceable solution. I feel that, in being party to this work, I have been a labourer in the cause of peace.

Questions

1. What part was played in the Egyptian Crisis of 1882 by (a) 'Bright' (Source C) and (b) 'Arabi' (Source D)? [4]
2. How do the content and tone of Sources A and B help to explain Gladstone's success as a leader of public opinion? [4]
3. How useful is Source C as evidence for policy making on imperial matters during the second Gladstone administration? [4]
*4. How fully does Source D explain British government policy towards Egypt in 1882? [5]
5. Using the sources and your own knowledge, explain why it was so difficult for Gladstone to realise the vision of international relations outlined in Sources A and B. [8]

Worked answer

*4. [This question asks for a critical evaluation of the source, in which Gladstone attempts to justify the actions of his government. You must show an awareness of the limitations of the source as historical evidence.]

In this letter Gladstone attempts to justify himself to a former colleague, John Bright, who had resigned from the government in protest at its decision to send troops to Egypt. Bright was a leading representative of the Manchester school of Liberalism, a believer in a peaceful, non-interventionist approach to foreign affairs. The source is therefore likely to stress the moral justification for using force in Egypt. Gladstone focuses on the threat to civil order posed by Colonel Arabi's rebellion. Britain has intervened to punish the violence of a military clique and has sought the backing of other countries for its actions. The source does not mention the issue of the Suez Canal's strategic significance, or the economic interests bound up with Britain's involvement in Egypt. One is left to assume that arguments based upon self-interest would have cut little ice with the recipient of the letter.

In some respects the extract could be regarded as a case of special pleading. The reference to 'the united Powers of Europe' is ironic in view of the fact that British intervention in Egypt was a unilateral action. Gladstone's pointed contrast between 'the civilised world' and 'the fanaticism of the East' is a surprising statement from the politician responsible for the internationalist rhetoric of the Midlothian campaign. Viewed as a whole, the extract testifies to the way in which ideals enunciated in opposition can be overborne by the everyday realities of power and responsibility.

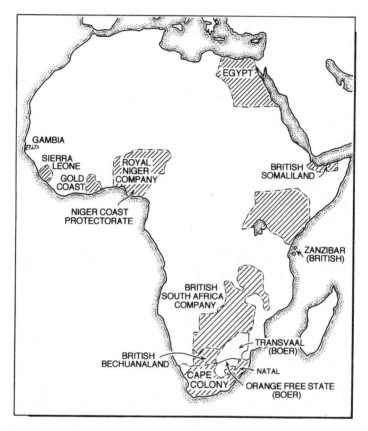

Map 2 British Possessions in Africa, 1895

3

A 'NEW IMPERIALISM'?

British overseas expansion in the late nineteenth century

BACKGROUND NARRATIVE

In the last two decades of the nineteenth century the major European powers engaged in a competition for territory in several parts of the underdeveloped world. More than one contemporary used the phrase a 'partition of the world' to describe this phenomenon, which affected the Pacific, the Far East and Africa. Of the powers 'scrambling' for empire, Britain emerged with the most substantial gains. It has been calculated that, between 1874 and 1902, Britain acquired an additional 4,750,000 square miles of territory, together with authority over almost 90 million people.[1] Her gains included the annexation of numerous South Pacific islands, the imposition of British authorities upon several Malay states and the conquest of Upper Burma.

It was in Africa, however, that the most striking advances were made. At the start of our period Britain's possessions in the 'Dark Continent' were relatively few and, where possible, she preferred informal influence to the political and financial burdens of direct control. In South Africa Britain had taken the Cape of Good Hope as a prize of the Napoleonic Wars. Natal, on the Cape's north-eastern border, had been acquired in 1843 with a view to strengthening Britain's presence on the shores of the Indian Ocean. In East Africa

British influence rested upon a commercial treaty with the Sultan of Zanzibar, an Arab potentate whose coastal domains occupied an important position on the trade route to India. Before the 1880s British involvement in the interior was minimal. Business interests had penetrated more extensively in West Africa. Here Britain possessed a handful of commercial territories between Gambia and the delta of the River Niger. Britain relied for the most part upon a network of relationships with local chieftains; outright annexations, such as that of Lagos in 1861, were exceptional. In common with most European powers, Britain was content to maintain an 'open door' for trade through collaboration with local leaders, supported by the threat of 'gunboat diplomacy' in the background. This was empire on the cheap, and by and large it was effective in securing regional influence for the imperial power.

After about 1880 the 'imperialism of free trade', as Jack Gallagher and Ronald Robinson termed it,[2] gave way to more formal control in many areas of the African continent. The occupation of Egypt in 1882 was at first presented as a limited intervention to restore good order and financial probity to a bankrupt province of the Ottoman Empire, but it steadily took on the character of a permanent occupation. In 1884–5 came the declaration of protectorates over the Somaliland in East Africa, and over Bechuanaland in the south. The granting of a royal charter to Sir George Goldie's Niger Company in 1886 was a preliminary to the establishment of two Nigerian protectorates thirteen years later. In 1889 Cecil Rhodes' British South Africa Company was chartered to extend British power northwards from Bechuanaland, into what would become Northern and Southern Rhodesia. In 1894–5 Uganda became a British possession and direct responsibility for Kenya was taken over from the Imperial British East Africa Company. The Sudan was conquered in 1898, enabling Britain to assume predominance in the whole of the Upper Nile region. It is not surprising that the search for explanations of these events should have generated a lively historiographical debate.

ANALYSIS: WHY DID BRITAIN PARTICIPATE IN THE 'SCRAMBLE FOR AFRICA' IN THE LAST TWO DECADES OF THE NINE-TEENTH CENTURY?

Lord Salisbury, who led Britain during the greater part of the 'scramble for Africa', remarked in 1891: 'I do not exactly know the cause of this sudden revolution. But there it is.'[3] He was not the only person to find it hard to explain the process whereby, in less than two decades, Britain became overlord of one-third of the African continent. The earliest and frequently the most politically committed writers tended to focus on the economic arguments for expansion. Others have interpreted the scramble as an extension overseas of European great power rivalries in the wake of German unification in 1870. A still more influential explanation stresses the importance of British strategic interests in Northern and Southern Africa. A further fault line divides commentators who emphasise the primacy of decisions taken at the centre – the so-called 'metropolitan' approach – from those who seek explanations on the periphery of empire among the administrators, the commercial and missionary pressure groups and African tribes and cultures.

The economic argument for African expansion was popularised in the early years of the twentieth century by the radical writer J.A. Hobson, author of *Imperialism: A Study* (1902). Hobson's theory derived from his belief that the domestic market in Britain had contracted as a result of the unequal distribution of industrial profits. Financiers therefore chose to invest their surplus capital abroad, where both the returns and the risks were greater. Imperial expansion arose when these financial interests induced the government to intervene abroad in order to protect their investments. Thus, in Hobson's words, 'finance is . . . the governor of the imperial engine, directing the energy and determining the work'.[4] The theory of 'under-consumption' has some validity for Southern Africa, where government involvement was certainly heightened following the discovery of diamonds close to Cape Colony in 1869. However, it seems to have limited application to other areas of Africa. The principal areas for British investment were the United States, Canada and Latin America. It has been estimated that seven-tenths of the total capital sent overseas between 1880 and 1914 was lent to Europeans transplanted abroad. Hobson's work was influenced strongly by his radical domestic agenda. One of the purposes of his critique of empire was to draw attention to the problem of low wages which, he argued, diminished the field for investment within the United Kingdom by restricting working-class purchasing power.

If the greater part of Africa was not, then, a lucrative zone for investment, it was certainly important as a source of raw materials for British industry. It is possible to explain British involvement in West Africa, for example, in these terms. The Niger region was an important source of palm oil, used in the soap, industrial lubrication and tinplate industries. Until the intensive exploitation of Malaya in the early twentieth century, it was also a leading supplier of rubber for tyres and electrical insulation. The great chocolate manufacturers, Rowntree of York and Cadbury of Birmingham, fuelled demand for Nigerian cocoa. From the early 1880s the growing interest of French and German trading rivals in West Africa led British merchants to demand government intervention. The establishment of the Oil Rivers protectorate in 1884 and the chartering of the Royal Niger Company two years later were responses to intense economic conflicts.

Nonetheless, as Ronald Hyam points out, one should be careful not to portray the British government as the passive tool of trading interests. Governments made their own assessments of the national needs of British commerce and were selective about the assumption of expensive formal commitments. The head of the African Department of the Foreign Office, Percy Anderson, underlined the pragmatism of British policy in discussing French penetration of the western coast in 1883: 'Protectorates are unwelcome burdens,' he wrote, 'but in this case, it is . . . a question between British protectorates, which would be unwelcome, and French protectorates, which would be fatal.'[5]

The relationship between government and chartered company was essentially a contractual one, in which the former sought to minimise its responsibility for administration. Thus the Royal Niger Company agreed 'to undertake all internal native wars and maintain order without charge on the Imperial Treasury while the Imperial Government contracts to defend the Chartered Company against the aggression of foreign powers'.[6] Technological development, especially in the fields of transport and weaponry, gave the companies a decisive edge over the capabilities of the native African tribes and reinforced a latent sense of Western racial superiority. Cecil Rhodes' buoyant claim that 'we are the first race in the world, and that the more of the world we inhabit the better it is for the human race'[7] strikes a modern reader as incredibly arrogant. The sentiment was underpinned by the knowledge that possession of the rapid-firing Maxim gun placed entire tribes at the mercy of relatively small numbers of European adventurers.

As this was empire on the cheap, it was also highly favoured by the home government. Only with the arrival of Joseph Chamberlain at the Colonial Office in 1895 did a senior British political figure think seriously of administering or developing tropical Africa at public expense. With his business background, Chamberlain viewed the Niger and Gold Coast hinterland as 'undeveloped estates', which a progressive imperial government should seek to exploit and improve. Yet even he was to meet resistance from a parsimonious Treasury when he sought to raise loans for colonial development. In any case, Chamberlain's activities do not help to explain Britain's initial involvement in tropical Africa.

An alternative interpretation, propounded by D.K. Fieldhouse and others in the 1950s and 1960s, views expansion in Africa as the projection of European rivalries into a new context. Supporters of this approach draw attention to the fact that the 'scramble' took place in the wake of important changes in the European balance of power following the Franco-Prussian War. In Fieldhouse's words, 'imperialism may best be seen as the extension into the periphery of the political struggle in Europe. At the centre the balance was so nicely adjusted that . . . no major change in the status or territory of either side was possible. Colonies thus became a means out of the impasse.'[8]

A variant on this theme was proposed by A.J.P. Taylor, who saw Bismarck as the key player in a strategy designed to prevent a Franco-British combination against Germany. Bismarck's statement that 'my map of Africa lies in Europe'[9] reveals his true priorities. Far from desiring colonies for their own sake, Bismarck entered the imperial game in order to draw closer to France. The means by which this was to be achieved was a quarrel with Britain over African territory in which Germany had hitherto shown little interest. By laying claim to imperial power status, Germany provoked Britain to expand in Africa.

It does seem that concern over German ambitions in Africa played some part in the calculations of British policy makers. Britain's annexation of Bechuanaland, for example, followed Germany's establishment of a protectorate over Angra Pequena, on the coast of South-west Africa, in 1884. Fear that Germany intended to link up with the Boer Transvaal republic, thus threatening the security of Cape Colony and Natal, prompted a British occupation of the unclaimed coastal territory between the two. As the Colonial Secretary, Lord Derby, wrote to a colleague: 'there is a difference between wanting new acquisitions and keeping what we have: both Natal and the Cape Colony would be endangered . . . if any foreign Power chose to claim possession of the coast lying between the two.'[10] A similar concern with German penetration of the Sultan of Zanzibar's dominions may explain the granting of a charter to the Imperial British East Africa Company in 1888, permitting it to administer and develop what would later become

Uganda and Kenya. Until then Sir William Mackinnon, who had founded the company as the East African Association, had striven in vain to attract government patronage.

It is noteworthy that, for all the intensity of their rivalry, the European powers usually contrived to settle their colonial disputes peacefully. The most ambitious example of this was the Berlin Conference of December 1884 on West Africa, at which ground rules for the partition of territory were worked out. The powers were required to prove 'effective occupation' and to inform their rivals before proceeding to annexation. According to Sir Edward Malet, who represented Britain at the talks, the aim was to help prevent 'the anarchy and lawlessness which must have resulted from the influx of traders of all nations into countries under no recognised form of government'. As Ronald Hyam argues, at the back of politicians' minds was the fear that by staking out increasingly confused rival claims, European powers might risk an outbreak of war among themselves. Native African rulers, for whom tribal conflicts were a fact of life, might support one European sphere of influence against another, thus dragging the imperial powers into mutual hostilities.[11]

This discussion of great power calculations leads naturally to consideration of the influential 'strategic argument' originally advanced by Ronald Robinson and Jack Gallagher. *Africa and the Victorians*, published in 1961, broke new ground by drawing attention to the way in which crises on the periphery of empire could help to shape the reactions of the 'official mind' at the centre. The book's starting point was the importance for Britain of the maritime routes to India and the East. According to Robinson and Gallagher, it was instability at the southern and northern tips of Africa that drew Britain into actions designed to secure the Suez Canal and the Cape route respectively. The decision to occupy Egypt in 1882 was taken by a British government that had come to view Colonel Arabi's nationalist revolt as a threat to the security of the canal. From this action, it is argued, flowed the other events of the 'scramble'. France responded to the British presence in Egypt by seeking compensation in West Africa. Germany extracted concessions elsewhere, exploiting Britain's dependence upon the consent of an international commission for its management of Egyptian finances. In the 1890s Britain's need to strengthen its hold upon Egypt drew it further up the Nile, involving it in the annexation of Uganda and the military conquest of the Sudan. Britain's security requirements thus provided the driving force behind expansion. 'From start to finish the partition of tropical Africa was driven by the persistent crisis in Egypt. When the British entered Cairo on their own, the

Scramble began; and as long as they stayed in Cairo, it continued until there was no more of Africa left to divide.'[12]

Robinson and Gallagher's thesis remains the most powerful challenge to the older economic interpretations of the scramble. It offers a plausible explanation of the British government's readiness in the late 1880s to interest itself in the commercially unpromising regions of East Africa. According to Robinson and Gallagher, economic development was 'more a consequence than a motive of the "Scramble". As an explanation of European rule in tropical Africa the theory of economic imperialism puts the trade before the flag, the capital before the conquest, the cart before the horse.'[13] Their emphasis on India's centrality to the thinking of British policy makers is well founded. By the 1880s India accounted for almost one-fifth of Britain's total overseas investment. It was the lynchpin of Britain's trade with Asia, a vital generator of revenue and a vast reservoir of military strength; in the words of Lord Salisbury, 'an English barracks in the Oriental seas'.[14] Communications with India constituted 'the spine of prosperity and security' for the empire,[15] and it is understandable that Britain should have gone to great lengths to protect them.

Yet another valuable insight of Robinson and Gallagher is their successful demonstration of the limited role played by popular pressure within Britain. Certain moments of high imperial drama, such as the death of General Gordon at Khartoum in 1885, could engage the passions of public opinion. A plethora of religious societies called stridently for government intervention to uphold the civilising mission of Western missionaries. Yet the evidence suggests that they had little practical influence on policy making. The shocking martyrdom of Bishop Hannington of East Africa in 1886 failed to change the Salisbury government's attitude to the region.

The annexation of Uganda had to await the arrival of a new government and a Foreign Secretary, Lord Rosebery, who was determined to override his colleagues' anti-interventionist prejudices. In order to make the case for annexation, he doctored a civil servant's memorandum on the subject and threatened resignation in order to secure a subsidy, necessary to delay the withdrawal of the ailing Imperial British East Africa Company. Finally, he 'improved' a report by Sir Gerald Portal, the commissioner responsible for investigating the situation. The eventual annexation was a tribute to Rosebery's persistence and was certainly not a foregone conclusion.

Nevertheless, the ideas of Robinson and Gallagher have not been received uncritically. It has been pointed out that the earliest stages of the scramble pre-dated the occupation of Egypt. France had initiated forward moves in Senegal in 1879 and Tunisia had been claimed in 1881. King Leopold II of Belgium had begun penetration of the Congo region in the early 1880s, independently of British action elsewhere in the continent. The 'Egyptocentric' argument of *Africa and the Victorians* has been criticised for attempting to make one factor bear too heavy a burden of explanation. More recent studies of the period have moved away from the emphasis of Robinson and Gallagher upon the cool calculations of the 'official mind' in London. J.M. MacKenzie, for example, characterises the scramble as 'a combination of exaggerated hope and over-heated anxiety'.[16] He explains it in terms of the conversion of a powerful and interlinked elite, composed of commercial, intellectual and official elements, to the dominant idea of imperialism. A variety of interests came to view the presumed opportunities offered by Africa as a solution to the economic pressures of the late nineteenth century. The lines between the business world and Whitehall became increasingly blurred as ties of social and family connection knitted together the disparate strands of the 'establishment'. Lord Aberdare, for example, who became chairman of the Royal Niger Company, was a former Home Secretary with considerable influence in the corridors of power.

In recent years an important variation on this theme has been offered in the work of P.J. Cain and A.G. Hopkins. Their interpretation is built around the concept of 'gentlemanly capitalism'. Cain and Hopkins are critical of older economic interpretations, which stress the importance of manufacturing interests in overseas expansion. Instead they emphasise the political influence of an elite based in the City of London and south-eastern England, deriving its wealth from the financial sector and closely linked to the landed interest. Whereas manufacturing entered a period of relative decline in the last quarter of the nineteenth century, finance and services continued to expand. They took advantage, moreover, of connections with the political elite which industrial interests had never enjoyed. Most historians have seen late Victorian Britain as a defensive power, conducting a rearguard action in the face of growing foreign competition. By contrast, Cain and Hopkins' perspective leads them to emphasise the continuing vitality of a state at the centre of the international financial system.

On this reading of events, the key element in the scramble for Africa was the growing interest of 'gentlemanly capitalism' in the continent. This was encouraged by the growth of regular steamship services after 1850 and the rise of large firms in the transactions sector, capable of running ships, financing large mining operations and advancing credit to local traders and producers. Cain and Hopkins argue that the intervention in Egypt was precipitated by the nationalist movement's attempt to gain control of the country's budget. The Suez Canal was not at first in danger and, in any case, the Admiralty gave priority to the Cape route until the 1890s. Britain was drawn into North Africa not by strategic considerations but by pressure to ensure that Egyptian debts were serviced.[17]

Not all historians accept these claims for the centrality of the City to imperial policy making. Cain and Hopkins' portrait of Britain as a still dynamic imperial power on the eve of the Great War remains controversial. The publication in 1998 of a substantial review volume, *Gentlemanly Capitalism and British Imperialism: The New Debate on Empire*, indicated that the subject was far from closed.[18] It is likely that the mechanics of the scramble for Africa will continue to arouse scholarly interest for some time to come.

Questions

1. Were strategic considerations more important than economic factors in promoting the scramble for Africa?
2. Did Robinson and Gallagher exaggerate the importance of Egypt in the scramble for Africa?

SOURCES

1. IMPERIAL POLICY IN EAST AFRICA

Source A: a memorandum by Clement Hill, a Foreign Office official, 20 October 1884.

The geographical position of the East Coast lays it more within the general area of our foreign policy than that of the West Coast. Our alternative route by the Cape to India may at any time make it important that we should have possession of, or at least free access to, good harbours: the importance is not less since the French movement in Madagascar. The Mahommedan element on the East Coast and the large Indian trade which is there carried on, with its connection, which if not close is none the less real, with all that concerns the Mahommedan world in the Soudan ... make it essential that we should secure a preponderating influence over its political future.

Commercially it has made great strides in the 10 years which have elapsed since the Slave export was checked and an impulse given to legitimate trade. Apart from the mineral wealth which is believed to exist between the coast and the great lakes, there is an unlimited capacity for the production of cattle, cereals, and all the usual articles of tropical trade.

Source B: Sir William Harcourt, Chancellor of the Exchequer in the fourth Gladstone government, argues against British involvement in Uganda, 20 September 1892.

I am very much exercised in my mind at the news from East Africa and Mombasa. As you will have observed the East African Company have 'thrown up the sponge' (being as I imagine insolvent), and a determined effort is being made to force the British government to take to the *damnosa haereditas* [cursed inheritance]. Rosebery has circulated a Memo. (for our consideration but not expressing his own sentiments), by Sir P. Anderson (of the F.O.), in the highest jingo tune advocating the annexation of the whole country up to the Albert Lakes with a view to the 'reconquest' of the Sudan via the Upper Nile . . . If we embark on this desperate business we shall have no end of trouble with the French and Germans, as indeed we already have . . . I see nothing but endless expense, trouble and disaster in prospect if we allow ourselves to *drift* into any sort of responsibility for this business, and devoutly hope we shall have nothing to do with it.

Source C: Sir Gerald Portal reports on East Africa for the Foreign Secretary, Lord Rosebery, August 1893.

Any other European power would be justified in taking the British place in Uganda if there is an evacuation, because of the Arab aspect of the problem . . . It is hardly possible that Uganda, the natural key to the Nile Valley . . . should be left unprotected and unnoticed by other Powers because an English Company has been unable to hold it and because Her Majesty's Government has been unwilling to interfere . . . All question of a complete evacuation of Uganda should be set aside.

Questions

1. Using Source A and your own knowledge, explain the importance attached by its author to 'Our alternative route by the Cape to India'. [4]
2. Explain the references to 'the highest jingo tune' (Source B) and 'an English Company' (Source C). [4]
3. What do the language and tone of Sources B and C reveal about the outlook of their respective authors? [6]
4. How reliable is Source B as evidence of British government attitudes towards imperial expansion in Africa in the 1890s? [4]
5. How complete a picture do these sources give of the factors influencing British policy in East Africa in the late nineteenth century? [7]

SOURCES

2. DIFFERING INTERPRETATIONS OF BRITISH INVOLVEMENT IN THE SCRAMBLE FOR AFRICA.

Source D: *The Economist* on the economic potential of Africa, 30 August 1890.

The trade of South Africa is in our hands and is considerable. The trade of the Lower Niger is also in our hands. But, apart from these, Algeria, Tunis and Egypt, are alone the countries of which the trade and finance are not really infinitesimal. There may be mining surprises in store. But the lands of tropical Africa are not usually suitable for a European population, and the present inhabitants are races which it must take a far longer time to civilise than those who look for immediate big results appear to think of. We do not, apart from surprises, look for any rapid development of either trade or financial success from these territories.

Source E: from a satirical poem by Hilaire Belloc, 'The Modern Traveller', published in 1898.

[The fictional character, William Blood, is the leader of an expedition against an African tribe.]

> I never shall forget the way
> That Blood upon this awful day
> Preserved us all from death.
> He stood upon a little mound,
> Cast his lethargic eyes around,
> And said beneath his breath:
> 'Whatever happens we have got
> The Maxim gun, and they have not.'

Source F: J.A. Hobson on the role of investment in overseas expansion, 1902.

It is not too much to say that the modern foreign policy of Great Britain has been primarily a struggle for profitable markets of investment. To a larger extent every year Great Britain has become a nation living upon tribute from abroad, and the classes who enjoy this tribute have had an ever-increasing incentive to employ the public policy, the public purse, and the public force to extend the field of their private investment, and to safeguard and improve their existing investments ... It is this economic condition of affairs that forms the taproot of

Imperialism. If the consuming public in this country raised its standard of consumption to keep pace with every rise of productive powers, there could be no excess of goods or capital clamorous to use Imperialism in order to find markets.

Source G: Ronald Robinson and Jack Gallagher on the causes of the partition of Africa, 1961.

By altering the European balance, the occupation of Egypt inflated the importance of trivial disputes in tropical Africa and set off a scramble. Quickened by the hope of prising the British out of Cairo, the French drove deep into west Africa, while the Germans took their opportunity to irrupt into east and west Africa, in an attempt to extort British support in Europe . . . Once the French and German governments for diplomatic purposes began to back their own traders against British firms, trade turned into a business of territorial claims. As long as the British remained trapped in Cairo, France and Germany had the opportunity and the incentive to challenge Britain in Africa.

In this roundabout way, the occupation of Egypt triggered off at last a secondary rivalry for possession of tropical Africa; and despite its small intrinsic value, began its partition among the Powers at the Berlin Conference of 1884-5.

Questions

1. Explain the references in Source G to 'the occupation of Egypt' and 'the Berlin Conference of 1884-5'. [4]
2. How would you explain the differing views of British overseas expansion given by Sources D and F? [5]
3. Which is more useful for an enquiry into the reasons for British overseas expansion in the late nineteenth century, Source D or Source F? [4]
*4. How reliable as an historical source is a literary work such as the narrative poem from which Source E is taken? [5]
5. How full a picture do these sources give of the reasons for Britain's involvement in the scramble for Africa? [7]

Worked answer

*4. [This question requires an appreciation of the particular extract and an awareness of the strengths and weaknesses of literary works as historical evidence.]

The last two lines of the extract neatly encapsulate one of the reasons for the success of British imperial initiatives in Africa. The reference to the rapid-firing Maxim gun stands for the technical and military advantages of European settlers over indigenous tribes. This example demonstrates the capacity of the literary form to present a topical issue in a memorable way. However, it is important to be aware of the bias of the author, who may not necessarily represent wider opinion. Moreover, the need to produce the work for sale to a mass market may involve some distortion of the truth. A poet (or novelist) is likely to place the entertainment value of the work above a responsibility for factual accuracy. In this particular case, the satirical intention of the author needs to be taken into account. The author has simplified a complex real-life situation for humorous effect. As numerous examples testify, from the Zulu War of 1879 to the South African conflict of 1899–1902, possession of superior fire-power did not always guarantee a rapid victory. Naturally, sober reflections of this kind cannot be allowed to intrude into a comic work.

4

'THE WEAKEST LINK IN THE IMPERIAL CHAIN'
Britain and the South African war of 1899–1902

BACKGROUND NARRATIVE

Nineteenth-century South African history was shaped by continual tension between the Dutch-speaking Boer or Afrikaner settlers, whose ancestors had arrived in the 1650s, and the more recently established British presence at the Cape. The Boers' determination to preserve their distinctive identity led them to undertake the 'Great Trek' into the interior in 1835–7. The settlements established by these trekkers were to be known as the Transvaal and the Orange Free State. Here the Boers nurtured their way of life, based upon pastoral farming, an austere Old Testament religion, a preference for republican government and the denial of political rights to the native black population. Their sense of nationalism developed in reaction to British attempts to incorporate the Transvaal in a South African federation in 1877. A brief military confrontation in 1880–1, known as the first Anglo-Boer War, culminated in a British defeat at Majuba Hill. This was followed by the restoration of the Transvaal's independence, subject to British oversight of its foreign policy, in the Pretoria Convention of 1881. Although this unusual arrangement was confirmed by the London Convention three years later, it remained a standing affront to Boer nationalists led by the Transvaal's fiercely independent President, Paul Kruger. From an opposite perspective, it was also viewed as an unhappy compromise by imperial-minded Britons. They sought full imperial control over the whole of Southern Africa.

In 1886 the discovery of gold in the Witwatersrand, an area of the Transvaal, transformed the economic potential of the Boer republic, enabling it to challenge the historic predominance of Cape Colony. In the next decade, the completion of the Delagoa Bay railway linked the Transvaal with the port of Lourenço Marques in Portuguese East Africa. This freed Kruger's regime from its dependence on British-held Cape Town for access to the sea. The gold rush drew in thousands of mainly British prospectors known as the 'uitlanders', who sought to make their fortune around the mining town of Johannesburg.

Fearing that they would be outnumbered by the newcomers, the Boers not only retained a monopoly of key materials such as dynamite but denied the uitlanders voting rights until they had been resident for fourteen years. In December 1895 Cecil Rhodes, Prime Minister of Cape Colony and chairman of the British South Africa Company, tried to wrest control of the Transvaal from the Boers by means of a settler uprising. In London, Joseph Chamberlain, Colonial Secretary in Lord Salisbury's government, gave covert and uncommitted support to the project. Although keen to undermine Boer political power, Chamberlain did not want to see an independent uitlander republic which might be no more friendly to imperial interests than the Kruger regime. In the event the rising failed to materialise and a foolhardy raid led by Rhodes' associate, Dr Leander Starr Jameson, ended in humiliation. Although Chamberlain's reputation survived the subsequent inquiry, the raid destroyed Rhodes' credibility and handed the Boers an unexpected propaganda success. It also won for the Transvaal the moral support of the Orange Free State and of Cape Colony's Dutch-speaking population, together with wider European sympathy.

In 1897 the arrival in Cape Colony of a new High Commissioner, Sir Alfred Milner, heralded a new and more assertive phase in imperial policy. Milner viewed South Africa as 'the weakest link in the imperial chain'[1] and was prepared to confront Kruger's government in order to secure British paramountcy. In particular he sought to present the political grievances of the uitlanders as a justification for imperial intervention. The killing of a British settler on the Rand, Tom Edgar, by a Boer policeman in December 1898 was magnified into a symbol of Transvaal government oppression. In a famous despatch to Chamberlain in April 1899, intended for publication, Milner melodramatically compared the settlers' lot to that of the 'helots', a class of slave in ancient Greece. At the end of May he met Kruger at Bloemfontein, capital of the Orange Free State. Kruger offered to halve the residential qualification for the uitlander franchise. Notwithstanding Chamberlain's advice that he should continue to negotiate, Milner was unaccommodating. The conference broke down on his insistence that the Boers should grant a five-year franchise qualification with immediate effect and that the Rand should receive a form of self-government. The Boer leader interpreted these demands as a bid for political domination: 'it is our country you want'. The Transvaal continued to build up its military forces and Milner requested reinforcements for the ten thousand British troops already in South Africa.

In August Kruger declared his readiness to accept the franchise conditions demanded at Bloemfontein. The offer was, however, qualified in two ways. Britain must abandon her claim to over-lordship and promise not to intervene in future on behalf of the settlers. In a speech later that month Chamberlain declared that Kruger 'dribbles out reforms like water from a squeezed sponge . . . The sands are running down in the glass.'[2] The assumption was that Kruger was playing for time and was not sincerely interested in a settlement favourable to uitlander and imperial interests. In September Britain decided to reinforce the garrison in Natal. In order to exploit the advantage of their current numerical superiority, the Transvaal and Orange Free State mobilised their forces. By October Chamberlain was preparing to issue an ultimatum when Kruger presented his own demand for the withdrawal of British forces. Shortly afterwards the Boer armies invaded Natal. The second Anglo-Boer War, often known as the South African War, had begun.

After severe initial reverses the British annexed the Boer republics in 1900. The Boers proved resourceful, however, in staving off final defeat by means of guerrilla tactics. British forces under

Field Marshal Roberts and General Kitchener resorted to the confinement of Boer women and children in concentration camps, a morally questionable tactic designed to deprive the enemy of their civilian support system. Peace was signed at Vereeniging in May 1902. Victory had been achieved at a terrible cost in terms of civilian lives and of consequent damage to Britain's international reputation.

In 1906–7 a new Liberal administration in Britain took the first steps towards the pacification of the Boer peoples by granting responsible government to the Transvaal and the Orange Free State. By 1910 both British and Boer leaders, for different reasons, had reached the conclusion that their interests would be best served by combining the various territories of Southern Africa into one unit. The outcome was the Union of South Africa, which joined Canada, Australia and New Zealand as a self-governing dominion within the British Empire.

ANALYSIS: HOW DID BRITAIN BECOME INVOLVED IN WAR IN SOUTH AFRICA IN 1899?

The Anglo-Boer War of 1899–1902 continues to attract historians' attention as a crucial test of Britain's imperial role. It is important not only for its impact upon Southern Africa but for the way in which its prolongation led to a widespread questioning of British institutions and national fibre. The conflict taught the imperial power, in Rudyard Kipling's famous phrase, 'no end of a lesson'. The arguments over 'national efficiency' which coloured Edwardian political debate were stimulated by failure to overcome Boer resistance rapidly and at low cost. In areas as diverse as defence planning, working-class health and social reform, the war helped to set the domestic agenda for the opening years of the new century.

Historians are at one in the importance that they attach to the war. Its origins, however, continue to be hotly debated. For example, scholars have begun tracing the beginning of their analysis from very different points in time. J.S. Marais' classic work began with the discovery of gold in 1886. Andrew Porter's study focuses on the diplomatic and political events of 1895–9, the first four years of Joseph Chamberlain's Colonial Secretaryship. More recently, Iain Smith has located the decisive turning point in the renewed assertion of British interests in the 1870s.[3]

The issue of dating is related to a deeper controversy between holders of opposing ideological positions. Early interpretations, by commentators sympathetic to the British side, saw the Boers as an obstructive force in the path of the imperial power's 'civilising mission'. They endorsed Alfred Milner's description of the conflict as an inevitable clash of opposing cultures: 'two wholly antagonistic systems – a medieval race oligarchy and a modern industrial state . . . cannot live permanently side by side in what is after all one country'.[4] A glance at the index of Cecil Headlam's carefully selected edition of Milner's papers reveals this kind of bias. The entries for the Transvaal include the following: 'despotic oligarchy of', 'unprogressiveness of', 'Government's policy a curse to South Africa'.[5]

Among those who favour explanations based upon the role of impersonal forces, the most influential have been advocates of an economic interpretation. J.A. Hobson placed the ambitions of the gold-mining magnates, the so-called Randlords, at the centre of his analysis. He linked the Jameson raid and the outbreak of war in a conspiracy organised by 'a small confederacy of international mine owners and speculators' determined 'to secure for the mines a cheap supply of adequate labour'.[6] Hobson's emphasis on the importance of minerals has been endorsed, from a Marxist perspective, by a number of later historians. Writing in the 1970s, Shula Marks and Stanley Trapido argued that the annexation of the Transvaal was motivated by a need to secure gold supplies for the British economy and to protect the interests of the mining industry.[7] The overthrow of Kruger's regime would satisfy the needs of the magnates. It would also ensure British control of the region's gold reserves at a time when shortages of this metal, so vital to Britain's international trading position, were anticipated. From a non-Marxist perspective, P.J. Cain and A.G. Hopkins have fitted Southern Africa into their thesis of 'gentlemanly capitalism', arguing that growing British investment there explains the urge to imperial expansion in the late nineteenth century.[8]

Economic interpretations continue to attract widespread support. Nigel Worden's 1994 synthesis of work on modern South African history stresses the political role of deep-level mining interests.[9] High production costs made these interests dependent on the recruitment of cheap, unskilled African labour and on favourable government policy. Frustrated by Transvaal taxes and monopolies, and denied the chance of exerting influence within the Afrikaner political system, the mine owners sought external aid. Their objective was a change of government that would protect their long-term interests in the Rand.

There are, however, problems with interpretations that ascribe such a major role to the magnates and to gold. Whereas it is easy to connect the Randlords to the Jameson raid, there is little evidence to support claims that they directly affected the decision for war. Indeed, it seems that the debacle of 1895–6 caused many senior figures in the mining houses to draw back from a damaging confrontation with the Transvaal authorities. As the research of Iain Smith and others has demonstrated, the Randlords' preference in 1899 was for a negotiated settlement.[10] Their work also underlines the lack of concrete evidence of links between British officialdom and mining or financial interests. Britain had no need to secure physical control over the gold of the Transvaal, and this was not the outcome of the war.[11] It has simply not been proved that the minds of the key decision makers in 1899 were focused on gold as a commodity in the international economy.

If the economic interpretation of the war is not fully satisfactory, does the answer lie in the political field, in the actions of the leading figures in Whitehall and the Cape? Thomas Pakenham, author of the standard narrative history of the war, is one of several historians to focus heavily on the relationship between Joseph Chamberlain in the Colonial Office and Sir Alfred Milner, Britain's 'man on the spot'. Milner is portrayed as a man driven by a sense of imperial mission, determined to annex the Boer republics and to integrate them into a wider federation of the white empire. Whereas Chamberlain sought to bring the Boers to conclude a settlement favourable to British interests, Milner's preference was for a straightforward takeover. The latter used his contacts in the British establishment to influence the Colonial Secretary, and deliberately limited the scope for compromise in his dealings with the Boer leaders. According to Pakenham, this was 'Milner's war', a conflict whose origins can be traced in essence to the inflexibility of a powerful proconsul.[12]

It is important, however, not to see these individuals as acting in isolation from wider political processes. To suggest that Milner dragged Chamberlain, and Chamberlain dragged a reluctant British government into war, requires a selective reading of correspondence from the period. As Ronald Hyam reminds us, this was a conflict of states, not of individuals.[13] Andrew Porter's research into the political background of the war has shown that Chamberlain enjoyed the steady support of the cabinet as a whole.[14] Although ministers expected Kruger to climb down without the need for war, the military option was contemplated from 1895 onwards. Salisbury and his senior colleagues were reluctant to incur the costs of overseas war, yet did not shrink from this when persuaded of its necessity. The Prime Minister was reported by a senior civil servant in October 1899 as 'prepared to face war sooner than not get out of Kruger terms that will secure good government at Johannesburg and make the Boers feel that we are and must be the paramount power in South Africa'.[15] Salisbury remained consistent in his defence of a forward policy, responding to critics of harsh British wartime methods that 'the Boers should have thought of [the war's] horrible significance when they invaded the Queen's dominions without a cause'.[16]

What, then, were the overriding interests that drove the imperial power to war? According to Robinson and Gallagher, the dominant factor was alarm at the challenge to traditional British predominance presented by an increasingly self-confident Afrikaner power. They explained the prominence given to uitlander political rights in the Transvaal in terms of Britain's need to nurture a community of local 'collaborators' to counterbalance Boer nationalism and uphold British influence.[17] This interpretation has been criticised by Andrew Porter, who has argued that Britain did not see the settlers as effective or trustworthy allies. The real significance of the uitlander franchise lay in the issue's 'democratic' resonance in late Victorian Britain. This gave it the status of a just cause, in whose interest British public sympathy and support could be enlisted.[18]

In both the public and the private statements of British ministers and officials, the position of the uitlanders was presented as a means to a larger end. Thus in a letter to Lord Selborne, the junior minister at the Colonial Office in July 1899, Milner noted that 'franchise and every other question have merged in one big issue; is British paramountcy to be vindicated or let slide?'[19] The need to uphold political predominance in the region was underlined by German penetration of Southern Africa in the 1890s. The Cape route to the East remained vital. Nor, for the sake of her prestige as a world power, could Britain allow herself to be defied by Boer intransigence. As Chamberlain expressed it in addressing the House of Commons, 'what is now at stake is the position of Great Britain in South Africa – and with it the estimate formed of our power and influence in our Colonies and throughout the world'.[20]

In explaining the centrality of Southern Africa to Britain's global strategy, several recent historians try to integrate political and economic factors. Andrew Porter, Iain Smith and others acknowledge the importance of mineral discoveries in transforming the economic potential of the Transvaal. Britain did not go to war to win control of the gold mines, but to prevent the Transvaal from using its newly found wealth to oust Britain as the dominant regional power. The cabinet's deliberations were shaped not by a wish to protect overseas investments, but by a need, in Salisbury's words, to demonstrate 'that we not the Dutch are Boss'. The growing assertiveness of Kruger's regime in the 1890s undermined the historic assumption of British policy makers, that Cape Colony would always be the centre of gravity in Southern Africa. Although Britain did not necessarily seek annexation of the Transvaal from the outset, the Boer republic certainly could not be permitted to draw the rest of the region away from traditional British influence. If war was necessary in order to re-establish that influence, then the imperial power was prepared to undertake it.

Questions

1. 'Milner's war'. Is there any validity in this description of the South African War of 1899–1902?
2. How would you distinguish between long- and short-term causes of the South African War of 1899–1902?

SOURCES

1. ANGLO-BOER RELATIONS 1895–8

Source A: Lord Salisbury discusses the Transvaal in a letter to Joseph Chamberlain, 30 December 1895.

It is evident sooner or later that State must be mainly governed by Englishmen: though we cannot yet precisely discern what their relations to the British Crown or Cape Colony will be ... but still it would be better if the revolution which transfers the Transvaal to British rulers were entirely the result of the action of internal forces, and not of Cecil Rhodes' intervention, or of ours.

Source B: Alfred Milner discusses the Dutch-speaking population of Cape Colony in his Graaff Reinet speech, 3 March 1898.

They loathe, very naturally and rightly, the idea of war, and they think that if they can only impress upon the British Government that in case of war with the Transvaal it would have a great number of its own subjects at least in sympathy against it, that is a way to prevent such a calamity. But in this they are totally wrong, for this policy rests on the assumption that Great Britain has some occult design on the independence of the Transvaal – that independence which it has itself given – and that it is seeking cases of quarrel in order to take that independence away ... So far from seeking cases of quarrel it is the constant desire of the British Government to avoid causes of quarrel, and not to take up lightly the complaints – and they are numerous – which reach it from British subjects within the Transvaal, for the very reason that it wishes to avoid even the semblance of interference in the internal affairs of that country ... That is Great Britain's moderate attitude, and she cannot be frightened out of it.

Source C: from a record made by Jan Christian Smuts, the Transvaal's Attorney-General, of a meeting with a British representative, J.G. Fraser, 23 December 1898.

He [Fraser] said that the British Government had now sat still for two years because her own officials had put her in a false position in the Jameson Raid. The time had now however come for her to take action. I asked him what he meant. He said that Gladstone had made a great mistake in giving the country back after Majuba before having defeated the Boers. The Boers throughout South Africa had a vague aspiration for a great republic throughout South Africa and that Gladstone had by his action encouraged this aspiration in them ... She [the South African Republic] would have nothing to do with the paramount influence of England but had always tried to play a role among the nations and had with a view to that always coquetted with the European powers. In his opinion the time had come to make an end of all this by showing the Boers that England is master in South Africa. I asked him what would give occasion for this. He said that England was very dissatisfied about the mal-administration and especially about ill-treatment of her subjects which was worse here than elsewhere. On this point England would take action.

Questions

1. Explain the references to (a) 'Cecil Rhodes' (Source A) and (b) 'Majuba' (Source C). [4]
*2. What does Source A reveal of its author's attitude towards British imperial policy making? [4]
3. How persuasive is Source B as a defence of Britain's South African policy at this time? [4]
4. Compare Sources B and C as evidence for the study of Anglo-Boer relations in this period. [6]
5. Using Sources A to C and your own knowledge, how far would you agree that responsibility for the deterioration of Anglo-Boer relations in this period was evenly divided between the two sides? [7]

Worked answer

*2. This source reveals Lord Salisbury, the British Prime Minister, as the advocate of a well-established, pragmatic approach to the extension of imperial influence and authority. He demonstrates flexibility regarding the exact nature of Britain's future relationship with the Transvaal, while making it clear that he wishes to see Britain emerge as the predominant power there. He also expresses a hope that 'internal forces' will act as the indirect agent of British policy in the region. An uprising by settlers on the Transvaal's gold fields would spare Britain the cost, in terms of both money and image, of direct intervention. Within days, the ignominious collapse of Dr Jameson's raid on the Transvaal, and the failure of the settler population to rise in revolt, would disappoint Salisbury's hopes.

SOURCES

2. THE APPROACH OF WAR, 1899

Source D: Alfred Milner writes to Joseph Chamberlain after the Bloemfontein Conference, 14 June 1899.

My proposals for a settlement of the Uitlander grievances on the basis of a moderate measure of enfranchisement having been rejected by the President, and a totally inadequate scheme put forward in their place, he now comes forward with an arbitration proposal. My contention is that the atmosphere in which that or any other concession to the S.A.R. [South African Republic or Transvaal] can be considered has yet to be created. Redress of the grievances of H.M. [Her Majesty's] subjects in the S.A.R. stands at the head of the programme, and nothing else can be considered till that matter is out of the way ... I cannot see the smallest reason why H.M. Government should not at once reject this particular proposal, and I advise that this course should be adopted.

Source E: Sir Henry Campbell-Bannerman, leader of the British Liberal Party, addresses the House of Commons, 18 July 1899.

[H]e could see no ground for surprise at the stubborn resistance made by the burghers, and especially by President Kruger, to the proposal to admit Outlanders [uitlanders] to the franchise ... the Boers had 'trekked' into the Transvaal to live by themselves, and now they felt themselves swamped by the newcomers, however much it increased their prosperity. Then there was the Jameson raid, which the Boers could not forget ... There was a certain strangeness in the idea that we should go to war to enable our fellow-citizens to give up their own citizenship in favour of another . . . at present there was no case, even for a threat . . . of war.

Source F: the government of the South African Republic states its terms, 16 August 1899.

The Government of the South African Republic . . . will assume that Her Majesty's Government will agree that a precedent shall not be formed by their intervention for similar action in the future, and that no future interference in the internal affairs of the Republic will take place contrary to the Convention. Further that Her Majesty's Government will not insist further upon the assertion of suzerainty, the controversy on this subject being tacitly allowed to drop.

Questions

1. Explain the references to the following: 'Uitlander' (Source D); 'the President' (Source D) and 'suzerainty' (Source F). [3]
2. What light does Source D shed on the reasons for the development of Anglo-Boer hostility? [5]
3. How reliable a picture of relations between Britain and the Transvaal would you expect Source E to provide? [5]
4. How do events in South African history after 1880 help to explain the demands made by the authors of Source F? [5]
*5. How complete a picture do these sources give of the reasons for the breakdown of Anglo-Boer relations in 1899? [7]

Worked answer

*5. [This question requires you to take a critical overview of all the sources, paying attention to what they omit as well as what they reveal.]

Sources D to F all suggest the important part played by the issue of uitlander political rights in the build up to the Anglo-Boer War. They do not, however, enable the reader to gain an objective view of the merits of the uitlander case or the extent to which it was manipulated for other ends. The only witness here to the crucial Bloemfontein Conference of May 1899 is Milner, who is seen by many historians as pursuing a deliberately provocative policy of his own. We are not given Chamberlain's reply and so have no way of telling how far Milner diverged from the preferred line of his political masters in London. Following the work of A.N. Porter and others, historians increasingly stress the importance of the British cabinet as a whole in the making of policy. The emphasis in Source D on the personal contacts between particular individuals hardly does justice to this perspective. The deeper issues at stake for Britain – of strategy, economic interest and great power status – are not reflected fully in this selection of sources. Moreover, although Source E is sympathetic to the Boer point of view, we are not given directly the attitude of Kruger and his advisers to the conference. Source F does not justify its claims with detailed reference to the immediate history of Anglo-Boer relations. An unrepresentative selection of diplomatic exchanges and partisan comments, divorced from the wider political context, cannot hope to give more than a limited view of a complex reality.

5

'SPLENDID ISOLATION'?
Lord Salisbury and foreign policy

BACKGROUND NARRATIVE

In the closing decade and a half of Queen Victoria's reign, the dominant figure in British foreign policy was Robert Cecil, third Marquess of Salisbury. Having served as Disraeli's Foreign Secretary in 1878–80, Salisbury went on to serve three times as Prime Minister (1885–6, 1886–92, 1895–1902). With the exception of two short periods (1886–7, 1900–2) he combined the Foreign Office with the premiership. In essentials Salisbury set the direction of Britain's overseas policies in these years.

During the two brief interludes of Liberal government in 1886 and 1892–5, the key figure was Lord Rosebery, a self-conscious exponent of 'continuity' in external relations. Gladstone, who finally retired from the premiership in 1894, tended to allow Rosebery a wide degree of independence. In any case the old man's declining energies were largely absorbed by the campaign for Irish Home Rule in his last two governments. As we saw in Chapter 2, in the closing stages of his career Gladstone failed to stem the tide flowing in favour of a more assertive approach to overseas affairs. In the 1890s a broad consensus between Conservatives and Liberal imperialists dominated official thinking on external policy making.

ANALYSIS (1): HOW EFFECTIVE WAS LORD SALISBURY'S HANDLING OF THE PROBLEMS HE FACED AS FOREIGN SECRETARY?

British policy in the Salisbury years was determined partly by the priorities of the Conservative governments but also by earlier events. Gladstone's occupation of Egypt created a source of enduring Anglo-French tension, while Russia's ambitions in the Near East and in the buffer states adjoining India were well known. These factors made it important, in Salisbury's first two administrations, for Britain to seek a working relationship with the Triple Alliance powers of Germany, Austria-Hungary and Italy. Throughout his tenure at the Foreign Office Salisbury remained wary of general agreements that might tie the hands of future policy makers. Nonetheless, in seeking to uphold specific British interests, he was always prepared to conclude limited arrangements with other powers. The important point was to avoid entering into open-ended commitments, which might work against British interests in unforeseen circumstances.

It was characteristic of Salisbury's unemotional pragmatism that, after failing in 1887 to negotiate a mutually acceptable plan for military withdrawal from Egypt, he thereafter accepted the reality of French hostility. Instead he sought security through a policy of 'leaning' towards the Triple Alliance without seeking membership. Salisbury's aim was to avoid a dangerous isolation while resisting the attempts of Bismarck's Germany to use Britain against France for its own purposes.

The Mediterranean agreements of February and December 1887 were a practical expression of Salisbury's strategy. The first of these, signed with Italy, was based upon a shared interest in opposing French ambitions in the Mediterranean and North Africa. Austria's later adherence enabled Britain to establish a connection to the Triple Alliance. The second agreement, which committed Britain, Italy and Austria to uphold the status quo in Bulgaria, Asia Minor and the Straits of Constantinople, was more specifically directed against Russian expansion. These agreements were not treaties as such; rather they took the form of an exchange of notes between the various governments. They therefore enabled Salisbury to maintain the flexibility that was the hallmark of his approach to foreign affairs.

In 1889 Salisbury turned down Bismarck's offer of a defensive alliance against France. Instead Britain underpinned her 'free hand' in European diplomacy by means of increased naval building. The Naval Defence Act enshrined the principle of the 'two-power standard', aiming to give Britain a margin of superiority at sea over the next two largest powers combined. The following year Salisbury negotiated the Heligoland Treaty, by which Britain handed over the North Sea island to Germany in exchange for the latter's abandonment of its claims to Zanzibar in East Africa. The agreement was motivated partly by a British desire to strengthen its hold on the southern approaches to the Nile Valley. By settling a potentially contentious colonial issue, it also enabled Britain to maintain diplomatic relations with Germany without entering a more comprehensive alliance.

In the next decade a number of factors made it harder to sustain the policy of limited alignment with the Triple Alliance powers. Kaiser William II's dismissal of Bismarck in March 1890 presaged a turning by Germany to a conscious policy of *Weltpolitik*, the pursuit of a global role at the expense of other powers. Episodes such as the 'Kruger telegram' of January 1896, when the Kaiser congratulated the Boer leader on surviving the Jameson raid, introduced a new sensitivity to Anglo-German relations.

Meanwhile, the conclusion of a Franco-Russian alliance in 1894 had serious implications for Salisbury's Mediterranean policy. This was demonstrated in 1895, when massacres of the Ottoman Empire's Armenian subjects provoked an outcry from British public opinion. Salisbury was caught between a political imperative to coerce the Turkish Sultan into reform and the strategic need to deter the Russians from using the crisis as an opportunity to seize the city and the Straits of Constantinople. The cabinet, however, impressed by the potential of the Franco-Russian combination, decided that the risk of war ruled out the deployment of Britain's fleet. At the same time Salisbury failed to enlist the support of the powers for a concerted attempt to enforce reform upon the Ottoman despotism. Sensing a shift in Britain's traditional Near Eastern policy, Austria insisted in January 1896 upon a binding military commitment to defend Constantinople against Russian intervention. Salisbury's inability to accept this new condition led to the non-renewal of the Mediterranean agreements and thus to the effective end of Britain's relationship with the Triple Alliance.

Withdrawal from the Straits of Constantinople increased the importance of Egypt for the defence of Britain's imperial communications, as the Admiralty came to envisage making a stand against the Russian fleet in the eastern Mediterranean. This shift in strategic thinking provided a powerful argument for the reconquest of the Sudan by General Kitchener's forces in 1896–8. This in turn increased the chances of a clash with France over control of the Upper Nile. In the Fashoda Incident of 1898, a British force was ordered to stand firm until a rival French expedition had been withdrawn from the region. The price was an indefinite delay for hopes of improved Anglo-French relations in general. The following year military reverses suffered by Britain in the Boer War tempted France and Russia to consider hostile intervention in collaboration with Germany.

The Boer War was one of a series of episodes that highlighted the exposed nature of Britain's international position. The Salisbury government's tame response to the United States' intervention in a boundary dispute between British Guiana and Venezuela in 1895 signalled acceptance of an inability to exert effective influence in all areas of the world. By accepting Washington's demand for submission of the issue to arbitration, Britain tacitly recognised the United States' dominance on the American continent. This led logically, in 1901, to Britain's renunciation of an earlier claim to share with the United States responsibility for the construction of a Panama canal.

More immediately significant was the challenge posed by her rivals in the Far East. British policy had traditionally rested on the principle of an 'open door' for European powers to pursue their trading interests in the decaying Chinese Empire. In 1898 Germany's seizure of Kiaochow, followed by further Russian penetration of Manchuria, raised the prospect of a scramble to partition China among the European powers. Britain's acquisition of a less important concession, the port of Weihaiwei, failed to allay fears in government circles that traditional diplomatic methods were inadequate in a changed situation. During Salisbury's absence through illness in 1898 the Colonial Secretary, Joseph Chamberlain, tried to improve Britain's position through unofficial approaches to Germany for an alliance. Chamberlain's initiative foundered, as did similar moves in 1899 and 1901, on Germany's unwillingness to assist Britain in curbing Russia's Far Eastern ambitions.

Germany's interest lay in an arrangement that would tie Britain to the defence of its land frontiers, not in an overseas commitment that would alienate its powerful Russian neighbour. Salisbury was clear on this point, writing of Germany's 'mortal terror on account of that long undefended frontier of hers on the Russian side. She will therefore never stand by us against Russia, but is always rather inclined to curry favour with Russia by throwing us over.'[1] Age and ill health compelled Salisbury to give ground to those of his colleagues who favoured further negotiations with Germany. It was with great reluctance that he consented to a deal with Germany in August 1898, whereby the two countries agreed to partition Portugal's African Empire in the event of its collapse. In November 1900 he relinquished the Foreign Office to

Lord Lansdowne, who was more open to the concept of definite external commitments. Yet Salisbury still retained the capacity to argue decisively. In a celebrated memorandum written in May 1901, he turned on its head the assumption that the Boer War underlined Britain's desperate need for allies. On the contrary, far from demonstrating the dangers of isolation, the war had revealed the inability of Britain's continental rivals to combine against her.

Nonetheless, Salisbury faced a powerful cabinet alliance in favour of some kind of adjustment in Britain's international position. Awareness of Britain's loss of predominance in the Mediterranean coincided with Russian penetration in China, central Asia and Persia. The rising costs of naval defence against threats on more than one front impressed themselves upon the Admiralty. This was the background to the Anglo-Japanese alliance of January 1902, the last major diplomatic event of Salisbury's administration and one about which he had serious reservations.

It seems that in his last two years in office, Salisbury's grip on policy was weakening to a significant degree. The memory of his twilight years should not, however, be allowed to detract from his record as a whole. To have guided British policy for so long, without involving the country in European conflict, was a considerable achievement. Those who criticise Salisbury for his reluctance to enter into binding general alliances should reflect on the implications for continental peace of the commitments made by Britain's rivals at the turn of the century.

Questions

1. How much did the success of Salisbury's foreign policy owe to favourable external circumstances?
2. How well were British interests served by Salisbury's Mediterranean policies between 1885 and 1896?

ANALYSIS (2): HOW ACCURATE IS THE TERM 'SPLENDID ISOLATION' AS A DESCRIPTION OF LORD SALISBURY'S FOREIGN POLICY?

The notion of 'isolation' as a description of British foreign policy in the age of Salisbury is one that enjoyed wide currency at the time. To some it was a conscious choice, which reflected Britain's ability to rely on her own resources and prestige as the head of the world's largest empire. Others saw Britain's lack of allies as an involuntary position, a source of weakness in the increasingly hostile world of the late nineteenth century. Thus in January 1896 the leader of the Canadian House of Commons referred to 'the great mother Empire . . . splendidly isolated in Europe', while an opponent in the same debate alleged that 'England stands dangerously isolated, and not splendidly isolated'.[2] It was possible to change one's mind about the merits of Britain's assumed detachment from continental alignments. Thus George Goschen, First Lord of the Admiralty, declared in a speech at Lewes in February 1896 that 'our isolation is not an isolation of weakness; it is deliberately chosen, the freedom to act as we choose in any circumstances that might arise'.[3] Yet in September 1900, conscious of Russia's penetration of China, Goschen acted as spokesman for a cabinet group who urged Salisbury to take steps 'to detach the German Emperor from Russia and bind him more closely to our interests'.

As C.H.D. Howard pointed out in a perceptive study, the concept of isolation, whether splendid or otherwise, was never clearly defined. Does it refer only to the avoidance of alliances with other great powers? Does it mean peacetime as opposed to wartime arrangements? In the nineteenth century the word 'alliance' often referred to a less close and formal relationship than those with which we have become familiar in the twentieth.[4] Most modern studies of Salisbury's diplomacy stress his readiness to co-operate with other powers where identifiable British interests were concerned. On assuming the premiership for the first time, in June 1885, he explicitly condemned the way in which the previous administration's policies had isolated Britain. 'The Liberal government have at least achieved their long desired "Concert of Europe" . . . they have succeeded in uniting the Continent of Europe – against England.'[5] In May 1898, speaking on the theme of 'living and dying nations', he referred dismissively to 'the jargon about isolation'.

Salisbury approached foreign policy making with an awareness of the limits as well as the potential of British power. With world-wide interests to defend and – unlike her continental rivals – no tradition of large-scale conscript armies, it was essential for Britain to avoid unduly provocative stances. Thus Salisbury was sceptical with regard to a Viceroy of India who favoured a 'forward' policy in reaction to Tsarist designs. 'Curzon always wants me to talk to Russia as if I had 500,000 men at my back, and I have not.'[6] The threat of war on more than one front seriously exercised Britain's military planners. The Director of Military Intelligence stated in 1887 that 'the countries with which we are most liable to go to war are France and Russia and the worst combination which we have any reason to dread is an alliance of France and Russia against us.'[7] Salisbury was well aware that naval power, although essential for policing the empire, had its limitations as a diplomatic asset. As he reflected on the first Mediterranean agreement, 'the interests of Austria and England coincided only at one point of momentous importance . . . nor can we be of much service to Austria if she is in real danger. What use should we be of, in repelling an enemy who came across the Carpathians?'[8] In any case rapid technological change in the last quarter of the nineteenth century meant that Britain's title to naval supremacy was rarely assured. The 1889 Naval Defence Act and the Spencer Programme initiated by the Liberal government in 1893 were responses to perceived weaknesses in Britain's defence provision.

Britain's circumstances dictated a coolly pragmatic assessment of challenges to national interests, and of the resources available to defend them. While upholding specific treaty commitments, it was necessary to avoid making promises that might oblige Britain to use force in an unpredictable future. In the words of J.A.S. Grenville, 'circumstances might alter and then, if the material interests of a nation should conflict with her written engagements, the latter would be of little consequence'.[9] It was a philosophy that pointed towards caution in international affairs rather than a strict detachment from other powers. If Britain were to enter into an engagement with another power, a definite return for the commitment was expected. For example, in 1887 Britain was prepared to support Italian interests in North Africa, in return for Austrian and Italian assistance in the maintenance of her position in the Mediterranean region. This explains Salisbury's readiness to enter the second Mediterranean agreement, described by A.J.P. Taylor as 'more nearly an alliance with a group of Great Powers than any Great Britain had ever made in time of peace and more formal than any agreement made with France or Russia twenty years later'.[10]

On the other hand, Salisbury had no hesitation in turning down an alliance proposal which was likely to involve Britain in unequal concessions to a foreign power. Bismarck's suggestion of an Anglo-German alliance in January 1889 was unappealing since it tried to commit Britain to Germany's anti-French strategy, without offering reciprocal aid in the event of Russian aggression against India. Similarly, in the spring of 1898 Germany offered no support for Britain's interests in China, yet expected Britain to tie herself to the Triple Alliance in Europe. Moreover, the Germans, conscious of their relative lack of imperial possessions, looked for colonial concessions as the price of their friendship. Characteristically, Salisbury denied that 'Germany had any claim that we should purchase her support by concessions to which, except for the consideration of that support, we should be averse'. Such diplomatic exchanges explain one historian's description of Salisbury as a keen lawyer protecting the interests of his client and determined to get the best bargain at a fair price in the market of international politics.[11]

The assessment of interests was not the only factor in Salisbury's policy-making calculations. He often cited sensitivity towards domestic political pressures as an explanation of his refusal to commit Britain to open-ended, long-term arrangements. Salisbury's parliamentary dependence on Liberal Unionist support, during his second adminis-tration, is often regarded as an example of this. Writing to Queen Victoria in the aftermath of the Home Rule crisis of 1886, he said of Britain: 'torn in two by a controversy which almost threatens her existence, she cannot in the present state of public opinion interfere with any decisive action abroad'. Salisbury's Liberal Unionist partners retained a traditional Liberal sympathy for France and an aversion to the authoritarian monarchies of the Triple Alliance.[12] Yet this feeling seems to have evaporated a decade later, when the cabinet's chief enthusiast for an Anglo-German alliance was the leading Liberal Unionist Joseph Chamberlain. Grenville suggests that the divergence between Salisbury and Chamberlain may have arisen in part from their differing perceptions of the Chinese Empire's commercial significance. With his business background, Chamberlain was inclined to attach more importance to the China trade than was a traditional diplomat of Salisbury's stamp.[13]

Throughout his years of power Salisbury argued that Britain's parliamentary constitution prevented governments from accepting binding agreements on behalf of their successors. This was a useful device for explaining to the leaders of authoritarian states his inability to undertake the extensive commitments that they pressed upon him. In his famous 1901 memorandum outlining his reasons for rejecting an Anglo-German alliance, he wrote that 'the British Government cannot undertake to declare war, for any purpose, unless it is a purpose of which the electors of this country would approve'. Britain could not 'invite nations to rely upon our aids in a struggle . . . when we have no means whatever of knowing what may be the humour of our people in circumstances which cannot be foreseen'.[14]

Yet where national interests dictated a different approach, this argument could be conveniently ignored. C.H.D. Howard cites an example from Salisbury's third administration of a British pledge to go to war in specific circumstances. This was the secret Anglo-Portuguese declaration of October 1899, undertaken at the start of the Boer War when it was essential to deny the Boers access to the sea via the Portuguese territory of Mozambique. In return for a Portuguese reaffirmation of a seventeenth-century commitment not to adhere to a treaty hostile to Britain, Salisbury confirmed an historic promise to defend Portugal's colonies. Nevertheless, it is fair to add that the declaration did not entail a new undertaking. Moreover, there was a qualitative difference between a pledge given to a relatively minor power like Portugal and a decision to join an international system like the Triple Alliance.[15]

A close examination of Salisbury's policies reveals the extent to which external pressures, as much as his own inclinations, inhibited him from working with other powers. It is worth recalling that it was Austria-Hungary, not Britain, who terminated the Mediterranean agreements in 1896. If Britain would not extend the scope of the agreements on their terms, the Austrians preferred to let them lapse. Nor was Salisbury's vain attempt to mobilise the 'concert of Europe' during the Armenian Crisis of 1895–6 remotely 'isolationist'. It was not his fault that other powers were reluctant to impose a reform programme on the Ottoman Empire. Salisbury hoped for overhaul of the corrupt Turkish system to make it more acceptable to its subjects or, failing that, a controlled partition of its territory. He considered this preferable to a 'free for all' in which Russia was likely to descend on the city and the Straits of Constantinople. It was unfortunate for Salisbury that the outbreak of war between Turkey and Greece in April 1897 revealed the Ottoman Empire's remarkable resilience and undermined his policy. Salisbury alone of European leaders had tried to stabilise the Near East by means of international co-operation.

With the passage of time, a generally favourable view of Salisbury's diplomacy has tended to emerge. His flexible approach to external problems proved a more effective guarantor of peace than the tight military alliances of Austria and Germany, France and Russia. As David Gillard has argued, the latter gave some guarantees for what happened in the early stages of war, while reducing the room for diplomatic efforts to avoid a conflict. The events of 1900–45 suggest that Britain's control over future events was limited, given the existence of other powers with weak interests in international stability.[16] By the end of the nineteenth century, with challenges to Britain's position in more than one part of the world, Salisbury's cautious policies aroused the impatience of many of his contemporaries. In retrospect, however, there is a great deal to be said for Salisbury's pragmatic concentration on the immediate interests of his country.

Questions

1. What considerations influenced Salisbury's conduct of foreign policy?
2. 'That brilliant, obstructive dead-weight at the top.' How far do you agree with Lord Curzon's assessment of Salisbury's conduct of foreign policy?

SOURCES

BRITAIN AND THE EUROPEAN POWERS, 1885–1902

Source A: from Salisbury's cabinet report to Queen Victoria on the first Mediterranean agreement, 10 February 1887.

It is as close an alliance as the Parliamentary character of our institutions will permit. Your Majesty's advisers recommend it on the whole as necessary in order to avoid serious danger. If, in the present grouping of nations, which Prince Bismarck tells us is now taking place, England was left out in isolation, it might well happen that the adversaries, who are coming against each other on the Continent, might treat the English Empire as divisible booty, by which their differences might be adjusted; and, though England could defend herself, it would be at fearful risk, and cost. The interests of Italy are so closely parallel to our own that we can combine with her safely.

Source B: from Salisbury's letter to Sir William White, British Ambassador at Constantinople, on the second Mediterranean agreement, 2 November 1887.

My own impression is that we must join, but I say it with regret. I think the time inopportune and we are merely rescuing Bismarck's somewhat endangered chestnuts . . . If he can get up a nice little fight between Russia and the three Powers, he will have leisure to make France a harmless neighbour for some time to come. It goes against me to be one of the Powers in that unscrupulous game. But a thorough understanding with Austria and Italy is so important to us that I do not like the idea of breaking it up on account of risks which may turn out to be imaginary.

Source C: from Joseph Chamberlain's speech at Birmingham, 13 May 1898.

One thing appears to me to be certain. If the policy of isolation, which has hitherto been the policy of this country, is to be maintained in the future, then the fate of the Chinese Empire may be, probably will be, hereafter decided without reference to our interests. If, on the other hand, we are determined to enforce the policy of the open door, to preserve an equal opportunity for trade with all our rivals, then we must not allow jingoes to drive us into a quarrel with all the world at the same time, and we must not reject the idea of an alliance with those Powers whose interests most nearly approximate to our own.

Source D: Salisbury's views on a proposal to join the Triple Alliance of Germany, Austria-Hungary and Italy. An extract from a confidential cabinet memorandum, 29 May 1901.

The liability of having to defend the German and Austrian frontiers against Russia is heavier than that of having to defend the British Isles against France. Even, therefore, in its most naked aspect the bargain would be a bad one for this country. Count Hatzfeldt [the German Ambassador] speaks of our 'isolation' as constituting a serious danger for us. Have we ever felt that danger practically? If we had succumbed in the revolutionary war, our fall would not have been due to our isolation. We had many allies, but they would not have saved us if the French Emperor [Napoleon I] had been able to command the Channel. Except during his reign we have never even been in danger; and, therefore, it is impossible for us to judge whether the 'isolation' under which we are supposed to suffer, does or does not contain in it any elements of peril. It would hardly be wise to incur novel and most onerous obligations, in order to guard against a danger in whose existence we have no historical reason for believing.
But . . . these are not by any means the weightiest objections that can be urged against [an Anglo-German alliance] . . . the British Government cannot undertake to declare war, for any purpose, unless it is a purpose of which the electors of this country would approve. If the Government promised to declare war for an object which did not commend itself to public opinion, the promise would be repudiated, and the Government would be turned out.

Questions

1. Explain the references to 'Prince Bismarck' (Source A) and 'the policy of the open door' (Source C). [2]
2. What did Salisbury mean by 'the present grouping of nations' (Source A)? How did this expose Britain to 'serious danger'? [4]
3. How useful is Source B as evidence for the formation of British policy in the Mediterranean region during Salisbury's second government? [5]
*4. How and why do Sources C and D differ regarding the

dangers of Britain's 'isolation'? How would you explain this difference? [7]

5. How useful are these sources in illustrating the factors that shaped foreign policy under Lord Salisbury? [7]

Worked answer

*4. [The answer requires outside knowledge of the topic as well as the extraction of information from the sources.]

Chamberlain emphasises the negative aspects of an isolated position. By implication he criticises the policies of the government to which he belonged, of which Salisbury was the head. Chamberlain was concerned about the Chinese Empire, which seemed very precarious in 1898 as a result of Russian and German penetration. Britain would lose her traditional access to Chinese markets if she persisted in a policy of detachment from European alliances. By contrast Salisbury did not believe that 'isolation' presented a serious danger to Britain. The country's victory in the Napoleonic Wars of 1803–15 was due to its geographical position (and, by implication, its naval strength) and not to a continental alliance. Salisbury was therefore not persuaded that there were good reasons for Britain to incur additional military commitments by joining the Triple Alliance.

The differences between the two sources arise in part from Salisbury's tendency to concentrate on Britain's immediate interests. Hence his choice of an historical analogy involving a real threat to Britain's physical security. It may be that Chamberlain's business background predisposed him to value Britain's commercial interests more highly than did the aristocratic Salisbury. Moreover, the latter professed a respect for constitutional practice which, he argued, prevented a British government from attempting to bind its successors to long-term military commitments. The dates of the two sources are also worthy of note. Chamberlain was speaking before the failure of an alliance initiative towards Germany. Salisbury, writing in 1901, had the benefit of this negative experience. Finally, a minister preparing a confidential memorandum for his colleagues is likely to speak more frankly about the realities of the situation than a politician seeking to influence a public audience.

6

'A DIPLOMATIC REVOLUTION'?

Edwardian Britain and the great powers

BACKGROUND NARRATIVE

During the first seven years of the twentieth century, Britain entered into three significant engagements with foreign powers: an alliance with Japan in 1902 and ententes, or understandings, with France in 1904 and Russia in 1907. The first two of these developments were associated with the replacement of Lord Salisbury by Lord Lansdowne as Foreign Secretary in November 1900. Lansdowne retained this office under the premiership of Salisbury's nephew and successor, Arthur Balfour, from 1902–5. Following the resignation of the Balfour government in December 1905, a Liberal administration led by Sir Henry Campbell-Bannerman came to power. The new Foreign Secretary, Sir Edward Grey, was to serve for exactly eleven years, becoming the longest-serving holder of that office in the twentieth century.

These changes of political leadership were accompanied by an increasing professionalism on the part of the Foreign Office. Zara Steiner's work has shown how the growing volume of diplomatic business promoted the development of a more sophisticated Whitehall machine, in which the senior officials enjoyed greater influence than had their predecessors.[1] Foremost among this new breed of civil servants were Charles Hardinge, who took over as Permanent Under Secretary in 1906, Sir Francis Bertie and Eyre Crowe. Whereas leading officials had traditionally been treated as little more than glorified clerks, Lansdowne and Grey allowed them to move beyond a purely administrative role. Although it would be an exaggeration to claim that they helped to determine policy, their advice certainly reinforced the basic attitudes of their political masters, especially in the case of Grey. Hardinge and his colleagues brought with them a suspicion of Germany's rising naval power and a readiness to seek firm connections with other powers.

ANALYSIS (1): WHY, AND WITH WHAT CONSEQUENCES, DID BRITISH GOVERNMENTS ESTABLISH LINKS WITH JAPAN, FRANCE AND RUSSIA BETWEEN 1902 AND 1907?

On taking office in November 1900 the new Foreign Secretary, Lord Lansdowne, thought initially in terms of reaching an accommodation with Germany. It took some time before he concluded that this was not a realistic objective. Shortly after entering the Foreign Office he wrote privately that he had few preconceived ideas, 'but I plead guilty to one – the idea that we should use every effort to maintain, and if we can to strengthen the good relations which at present exist between the Queen's Government and that of the [German] Emperor'.[2] His main concern was to find a partner for the task of checking Russian ambitions in Central Asia and, more immediately, in Manchuria and other parts of the Far East. Intensive discussions in the spring of 1901 demonstrated the impossibility of an Anglo-German alliance. The Germans would not endanger their security in Europe by antagonising Russia in China, an area where they lacked vital interests.

Failure to find common ground with Germany, and to reach an accommodation with Russia, drove Lansdowne in the direction of Japan. The First Lord of the Admiralty, Lord Selborne, provided a powerful argument for an Anglo-Japanese alliance by drawing attention to the financial strains of attempting to uphold a two-power naval standard. Britain's fleet in Chinese waters was outnumbered by those of France and Russia. If Britain were to divert ships to that region, it would leave her dangerously vulnerable to attack in home waters and the Mediterranean. The twin pressures of security and economy dictated a diplomatic initiative to enlist Japan's help in defending the status quo in the Far East. Lansdowne met cabinet critics of such a proposal with the argument that an Anglo-Japanese alliance would reduce the chances of Japan forging links with Russia. It would also deter Russian expansion and make the Tsarist regime more likely to see the good sense of an agreement with Britain.

The agreement with Japan was not finalised without some differences of perspective between the two partners. Japan's primary interest lay in establishing Korea as a sphere of influence and its leaders had not ruled out the possibility of a confrontation with Russia in the region. Lansdowne and his colleagues were uneasy about allowing Japan total freedom to take any steps necessary to 'safeguard and promote' its position in Korea. In his last major foreign policy statement before retirement, Salisbury cautioned against giving Japan the right to commit Britain to a war of which she might not approve. He raised the spectre of Britain yielding 'without reserve into the hands of another power the right of deciding whether we shall or shall not stake the resources of the Empire on the issue of a mighty conflict'.[3] Ministers also objected to the Japanese demand that Britain should maintain a naval force equal to that of any other power in the Far East. After all, the point of the agreement, as far as the Admiralty was concerned, was to facilitate the concentration of the Royal Navy in European waters. Ultimately criticism on both counts was quietened by some rather ambiguous modifications to the text of the agreement, and the Anglo-Japanese alliance was signed in January 1902.

The alliance covered only the Far East and was signed initially for a five-year period. Its main proviso was that Britain would be neutral in a war between Japan and one other power, but would give assistance if Japan faced more than one opponent. Japan committed herself to identical obligations. Thus Britain was able to avoid involvement in war when smouldering Russo-Japanese rivalry exploded into open conflict in February 1904. Although Japan emerged victorious from the war, Lansdowne and his colleagues continued to fear Russian expansion in Central Asia. Concern for the security of India encouraged Lansdowne to press for the renewal of the Japanese alliance in 1905, well ahead of its expiry date. The outcome was an extension of the original treaty, whereby each party pledged to support the other if attacked by one other power. By enlisting Japanese assistance for the task of defending the Indian frontier the alliance achieved, on paper at least, one of the major objectives of Lansdowne's foreign policy.

France was the second great power with which Britain established formal ties during Lansdowne's tenure at the Foreign Office. The celebrated Entente Cordiale of April 1904, preceded by an exchange of state visits by King Edward VII and President Loubet, centred on the resolution of several outstanding colonial disputes. As we have seen, the British occupation of Egypt had been a running sore in cross-Channel relations since 1882. On the other side, Britain had declined to recognise the primacy of French interests in Morocco, where France was competing for influence with Italy and Spain. It took some time before the French government was prepared to contemplate linking the Egyptian and Moroccan issues as the basis of a deal with Britain. The memory of France's humiliation in the Fashoda Incident of 1898 made an understanding with Britain sensible while simultaneously creating a psychological barrier to such a development.

The 1904 understanding consisted of a series of pragmatic colonial bargains between the two rivals. In return for recognition of her solitary stewardship in Egypt, Britain accepted French primacy in Morocco. In the Far East Siam (modern Thailand) was acknowledged as a buffer zone between British Burma and French Indo-China. A deal was reached on another contentious point, the question of fishing rights off Newfoundland. Joint administration of the New Hebrides was agreed and Britain relinquished all claims to Madagascar.

For Balfour and Lansdowne, the purpose of the entente was primarily to ease Britain's global position and to pave the way for an understanding with France's ally, Russia. Nonetheless, its conclusion undoubtedly encouraged the increasingly vocal and influential section of opinion that viewed Kaiser William II's Germany as Britain's most likely antagonist. This was the priority of important elements in the Foreign Office, the Admiralty and the right-wing press. In 1902 the government had accepted an Admiralty proposal to build a North Sea base, the size of which would be 'practically determined by the power of the German Navy'. The following year Lansdowne had been compelled by parliamentary and public hostility to withdraw from co-operation with Berlin in the Baghdad railway-building project. The entente was welcomed by those who saw the rise of German navalism as the principal threat to national security.

By the same token it was viewed in a negative light by the German government, which set out in March 1905 to undermine the entente by challenging French claims to Morocco. The Kaiser staged a landing at Tangier and asserted the country's independence. Germany's intention was to expose the hollowness of the entente by compelling France to surrender, unsupported by its British partner. The crisis brought down the French Foreign Minister, Delcassé, negotiator of the entente, whose colleagues considered his stance on Morocco to be too hard-line. However, through the support of the British, the French government avoided an unconditional acceptance of the German demands. Lansdowne averted the collapse of the entente without being forced to make a more extensive commitment to supporting France. He achieved this by means of a veiled threat to the German Ambassador, that in the event of a Franco-German clash, 'it could not be foreseen how far public opinion in England would drive the government to support France'.[4] The face-saving device of an international conference at Algeçiras provided a vehicle for Germany's abandonment of its challenge to France in Morocco.

By the end of 1905 there had been a change of government. The new Foreign Secretary, Sir Edward Grey, had made it clear before taking office that the Anglo-French entente was fundamental to British policy. In a speech delivered in October 1905 he had stated that 'nothing we do in our relations with Germany is in any way to impair our existing good relations with France.'[5] Grey maintained continuity with his predecessor by warning that an unprovoked German attack on France would create a climate of opinion in which it would be 'impossible for England to remain neutral'. In January 1906 he also gave his backing to the first of a series of Anglo-French military conversations. Known only to a handful of ministers at first, these talks were to assume considerable significance. At the same time Grey insisted that Britain was not legally committed to the defence of France and that the political question of intervention in a European conflict remained open.

The new Foreign Secretary also embraced the concept of a rapprochement with Russia, whose position had altered a great deal since the abortive talks undertaken by the Conservative government in 1901. Defeat in the Russo-Japanese War of 1904–5 had forced a retreat from Manchuria. Britain's renewal of the Japanese treaty in 1905 provided a powerful argument against Russian military action on the Indian frontier. By August 1907 the Tsarist regime was ready to come to terms with Britain on a range of outstanding issues. The two powers agreed to recognise China's authority in Tibet, which was to remain independent. Russia accepted Afghanistan as a British sphere of influence, while Britain promised not to interfere in its internal affairs. Persia (modern Iran) was divided into three zones: a British zone in the south-eastern area close to the Indian border, a Russian one in the north and a neutral area in the centre.

The agreement brought some relief to the problem of defending India. As the Secretary for India, John Morley, warned the Viceroy, Lord Minto, 'what a tremendous load of military charge and responsibility you have to carry if you won't come to terms diplomatically with Russia'.[6] It was achieved in the teeth of backbench radical Liberal opposition to any accommodation with Tsarist despotism. The agreement also aroused the anger of imperialists such as the former Viceroy of India, Lord Curzon, whose preference was for a 'forward' policy against Russia: 'it gives up all that we have been fighting for for years . . . the efforts of a century sacrificed and nothing or next to nothing in return'.[7] Certainly, the Persian section of the agreement gave a significant advantage to Russia and failed to prevent renewed controversy over that country four years later. The entente signalled a more reasonable approach by both powers to their differences. Its authors did not expect it to eliminate entirely the historic mistrust that lay between the signatories. In that respect their assessment of future probabilities turned out to be a realistic one.

Questions

1. What pressures brought about the Anglo-Japanese alliance of 1902?
2. Were the ententes with France and Russia anything more than superficial arrangements, concluded with little expectation of long-term relations?

ANALYSIS (2): DID BRITISH FOREIGN POLICY UNDERGO A 'DIPLOMATIC REVOLUTION' IN THE PERIOD 1902–7?

The authors of the international agreements concluded in the period 1902–7 were conscious of breaking with past traditions of British foreign policy. In commending the Anglo-Japanese treaty to the House of Lords, Lansdowne appealed to his audience not to allow 'their judgement to be swayed by any musty formulas or old-fashioned superstitions as to the desirability of pursuing a policy of isolation'. On the other side, Sir William Harcourt, representative of the 'little England' section of the Liberal Party, declared that the alliance meant 'the departure from principles which have been consecrated by the traditions of nearly a century'.[8] Sir Edward Grey saw the subsequent agreements with France and Russia in the same light. Writing in September 1907, he pointed to the dangers entailed in any departure from Britain's understanding with France: 'we shall run the risk of returning to our position of nervous isolation in Europe, and of losing much of the strong position which our recent policy has won for us'.[9]

Traditionally most historians endorsed the belief that the Lansdowne–Grey period witnessed a fundamental reorientation of

Britain's foreign policy. Harold Temperley and Lillian Penson, two lead-ing authorities of the 1930s, described the Anglo-Japanese Treaty as 'revolutionary, a departure not only from the principles of Salisbury but even from those of Canning, which deprecated increase of obligations by guarantees or alliances'.[10] More recently, however, historians have tended to emphasise the essential continuity of Edwardian diplomacy. As we saw in Chapter 5, the old view of Salisbury as pursuing a policy of 'splendid isolation' now commands little support. Thus C.J. Lowe has argued that Britain was as close to the Triple Alliance in 1886–97 as to France and Russia in 1903–14. The collapse of Britain's relationship with Austria-Hungary and Italy after 1897 was not the result of a turning towards isolationism on the part of the British government.[11] Similarly, in his survey of British external policy in the twentieth century David Reynolds warns against viewing the ententes of 1904 and 1907 as embryonic military alliances. Rather they formed part of a continuing 'search for the elusive balance' in foreign relations and thus represented an extension of earlier policies.[12]

The argument for continuity is not, in fact, wholly new. At the time of the Anglo-Japanese alliance, Salisbury's son, Lord Cranborne, wrote that 'for the last twenty years we have been engaged with different Powers, notably with Germany and with France, in adjusting conflicting claims, and in bargaining so as to get rid of causes of friction'.[13] At first sight this seems to be at odds with the opinion of Salisbury himself as expressed in his memorandum of 7 January 1902. Writing of the risk of being dragged into war by Japanese actions in Korea or China, he warned that 'there is no limit: and no escape. We are pledged to war, though the conduct of our ally may have been followed in spite of our strongest remonstrances, and may be avowedly regarded by us with clear disapprobation.'[14] Sir Michael Hicks-Beach, the Chancellor of the Exchequer and Salisbury's closest cabinet ally, maintained that the Japanese treaty would not have been signed had the latter still been Foreign Secretary.

Nevertheless, Salisbury's memorandum does not betray the same fundamental hostility which he had displayed towards the proposals for an Anglo-German alliance the previous year. It should be remembered that he gave his consent to the signing of the Japanese treaty. As Ian Nish, author of a detailed study of Anglo-Japanese relations argues, the Prime Minister's words are best seen as constructive criticism of a draft treaty. Although the treaty entailed serious commitments, these were geographically limited to the Far East and were less sweeping than in the case of a European alliance. Nish sees the alliance as a modest departure from tradition, part of a gradual process of adjustment to

Britain's changed status in the world.[15] In this he is close to A.J.P. Taylor's argument that 'the alliance did not mark the end of British isolation: rather, it confirmed it. Isolation meant aloofness from the European balance of power; and this was now more possible than before.'[16] By giving Britain a partner in the Far East, the alliance destroyed the rationale behind the earlier quest for German friendship and thus increased her freedom to stand aloof, if she chose, from continental affairs.

In another sense, however, the Japanese alliance made it harder to keep Britain's Eastern and European policies separate. The terms of the 1902 treaty and of the 1894 Franco-Russian alliance obliged the participants to aid each other against two or more enemies. This meant that in the event of a Russo-Japanese war, both Britain and France had a strong interest in persuading each other to stay out. If they failed to resolve their differences, they faced the possibility of becoming involved in a conflict that did not concern them directly. The Anglo-Japanese alliance therefore indirectly helped to push Britain and France towards the Entente Cordiale.

With the conclusion of the latter Britain had taken the plunge into a public rapprochement with a major European power. Yet one should not allow the shadow of 1914 to induce an overly deterministic reading of previous history. The diplomatic history of the pre-war decade should not be viewed simply in terms of an irreversible commitment to an anti-German continental coalition. The Anglo-French and Anglo-Russian ententes were primarily designed to settle past disputes in the interests of wider security. In spite of growing concern at the rise of German power, neither agreement was specifically directed against it. Lansdowne continued to regret his inability to reach an accommodation with Germany. Together with important sections of the British establishment, he and Balfour showed more concern in 1902–5 with the Russian threat in Central Asia than with Germany.

It was the perceived aggression of Germany, in the Morocco Crisis of 1905–6, that tightened the bonds of the Anglo-French entente and caused it to take on an increasingly defensive character. When the entente was concluded, France's own security rested on the alliance with Russia and her association with Britain was not seen as relevant to her anti-German strategy. However, Russia's defeat at the hands of Japan in 1905 cast doubt on the value of the former as an ally in war. External events thus drove the French to press for closer links with Britain than they had originally envisaged. Yet there was no guarantee that the British would be willing to move beyond their limited commitment to continental affairs.

As Foreign Secretary, Grey hoped that his diplomacy would form the basis of a new European concert which would contain German ambitions and thus maintain a balance of power. This was consistent with his statement, made a few weeks after taking office, that 'an entente between Russia, France and ourselves would be absolutely secure. If it is necessary to check Germany it could then be done.'[17] Grey steadfastly resisted French pressure to turn the entente into a military alliance. As late as 1912 the British government was prepared to send the Secretary for War, Haldane, to Germany to offer an agreement on naval construction together with the prospect of colonial concessions. Yet Grey's policy would be meaningless if he allowed it to be assumed that Britain would stand aloof in the event of German aggression against France. As H.H. Asquith, Prime Minister from 1908, put it: 'nothing, I believe, would meet [Germany's] purpose which falls short of a promise on our part of neutrality: a promise we cannot give'.[18] The authors of the ententes did not intend a 'diplomatic revolution' to result from their actions. Yet in the context of German behaviour in 1905–14, these undertakings worked to limit Britain's freedom of action in a way that could not have been imagined.

Questions

1. Did the Anglo-Japanese alliance of 1902 tend to increase or restrict Britain's involvement in European affairs?
2. 'An entente is stronger than an alliance, because it is not defined' (Lord Lansdowne, 1 August 1914). Discuss with reference to the 1904 Anglo-French entente and the 1907 Anglo-Russian entente.

SOURCES

RELATIONS WITH JAPAN, FRANCE AND GERMANY, 1902–5

Source A: Lord Lansdowne to Sir Claude Macdonald on the signing of the Anglo-Japanese alliance, 30 January 1902.

We have thought it desirable to record in the Preamble of the instrument the main objects of our common policy in the Far East, and in the first Article we join in entirely disclaiming any aggressive tendencies either in China or Corea [Korea]. We have, however, thought it necessary also to place on record the view entertained by both the high contracting parties that should their interests, as above described, be endangered, it will be admissible for either of them to take such measures as may be indispensable in order to safeguard those interests.

The principal obligations undertaken mutually are those of maintaining a strict neutrality in the event of either of them becoming involved in war, and of coming to one another's assistance in the event of either of them being confronted by the opposition of more than one hostile Power.

HMG [His Majesty's Government] have been largely influenced in their decision to enter into this important contract by the conviction that it contains no provisions which can be regarded as an indication of aggressive or self-seeking tendencies in the regions to which it applies. It has been concluded purely as a measure of precaution to be invoked, should occasion arise, in the defence of important British interests.

Source B: Lord Cromer to Lord Lansdowne, 17 July 1903.

What it really amounts to is this: that everything depends on our attitude as regards Morocco. M. Delcassé, you say, 'did not attempt to disguise from me the immense importance which the French Government attached to obtaining from us a recognition of the predominance which they desired to obtain in Morocco.' I rather anticipated something of this sort, but I certainly did not expect M. Delcassé to go so far as to say that 'he was entirely in favour of a comprehensive settlement, and that the Egyptian formed part of the larger African question, which could, he felt sure, be disposed of satisfactorily if only we could come to an agreement as to the position of France in Morocco.'

Source C: A report of A.J. Balfour's words to the British Cabinet, 8 June 1905.

Mr Balfour pointed out that M. Delcassé's dismissal or resignation under pressure from the German Government displayed a weakness on the part of France which indicated that she could not at present be counted on as an effective force in international politics. She could no longer be trusted not to yield to threats at the critical moment of a negotiation. If therefore Germany is really desirous of obtaining a port on the coast of Morocco, and if such a proceeding be a menace to our interests, it must be to other means than French assistance that we must look for our protection.

Questions

1. Explain the references to 'Lord Lansdowne' (Source A) and 'M. Delcassé' (Source B). [2]
2. From your knowledge of Anglo-French relations in the preceding twenty years, why did the author of Source B not

expect 'M. Delcassé' to say that he was 'entirely in favour of a comprehensive settlement, and that the Egyptian formed part of the larger African question'? [5]

*3. Using your own knowledge of the events of 1905, explain the reference in Source C to 'M. Delcassé's dismissal or resignation under pressure from the German Government'. How was the crisis to which Balfour refers eventually resolved? [7]

4. Evaluate the usefulness of Source C for a student of British foreign policy during the Balfour government. [5]

5. Does the evidence of these sources support the claim that British foreign policy in this period 'sought the maximum advantage in return for the minimum commitment'? [6]

Worked answer

*3. The phrase refers to the behaviour of Germany following the conclusion of the Anglo-French entente. In March 1905 the German government attempted to humiliate France by challenging its claim to be the predominant imperial power in Morocco. The expectation was that France, finding that Britain would not give its support, would be forced to abandon this claim. In this way the fragility of the entente would be exposed. Kaiser William II therefore visited Morocco and asserted its status as an independent state. In France Delcassé, the author of the entente, was forced to resign. The crisis was resolved, and the French spared from further humiliation, by the British government's support for an international conference at Algeçiras. Lord Lansdowne warned the German Ambassador that British public opinion could not be counted upon to remain neutral in a conflict between France and Germany. Notwithstanding the scepticism expressed by Balfour in this extract, this action demonstrated Britain's continued commitment to the entente with France. This policy, moreover, commanded bipartisan support. In December 1905 the Balfour government had given place to that of the Liberal leader, Sir Henry Campbell-Bannerman, whose Foreign Secretary, Sir Edward Grey, pursued the same broad approach as his predecessor.

7

'THE LAMPS ARE GOING OUT'

Sir Edward Grey and the growth of
Anglo-German rivalry

BACKGROUND NARRATIVE

The Liberal government that took Britain into the Great War,
in August 1914, was led by H.H. Asquith. Like his predecessor
as Prime Minister, Sir Henry Campbell-Bannerman, he constructed
a cabinet whose membership reflected the various strands of party
opinion. Together with Sir Edward Grey, the Foreign Secretary, and
Richard Haldane, who moved from the War Office to the Lord
Chancellorship in 1912, Asquith represented the party's 'Liberal
imperialist' wing. Winston Churchill, First Lord of the Admiralty
from 1911, shared their commitment to strong defence and a
'patriotic' role for Britain. The pacific, Gladstonian tradition was
represented by Lord Loreburn, who retired as Lord Chancellor in
1912, and by Lord Morley and John Burns, who were still in office
on the eve of the war. Most members of the cabinet occupied a
moderate position, somewhere between these ideological opposites.
The most important 'uncommitted' figure was the Chancellor of
the Exchequer, David Lloyd George, who had acquired an early
reputation as an anti-militarist, social-reforming radical. From
about 1911 he was to assume a more assertive stance in relation to
external affairs.

As we saw in Chapter 6, Grey was strongly committed to support for the Anglo-French entente against the rising power of Germany. In this he was supported by his most important Civil Service advisers in Whitehall. A suspicion of German designs and a determination to uphold what he saw as vital British interests on the European continent were to be hallmarks of Grey's tenure at the Foreign Office.

ANALYSIS (1): HOW FAR DID ANGLO-GERMAN RIVALRY INFLUENCE THE CONDUCT OF POLICY UNDER SIR EDWARD GREY?

By the time that Sir Edward Grey took office, concern at Germany's growth as an economic competitor had been reinforced by a keen sense of rivalry in naval building. From the late 1890s Admiral Tirpitz, Kaiser William II's Secretary of State for the Navy, pursued a determined programme of battleship construction, linked to the progressive replacement of older vessels. It seemed that the Germans were consciously seeking to replace Britain as the world's leading naval power. Certainly, Tirpitz aimed to increase the size of the German fleet to a level where it could inflict such heavy losses that no adversary would contemplate an attack upon it. British alarm over the German challenge in the North Sea was the main factor behind the launching in 1906 of HMS *Dreadnought*, a new, all big-gun battleship whose appearance effectively rendered all rivals obsolete. The decision to concentrate the greater part of the British fleet in home waters from that year was taken with the same consideration in mind. Equally significant was the tacit acknowledgement that the two-power standard, the basis of British policy since 1889, was no longer applicable. The Liberal government wanted to make savings where it could, in order to make possible ambitious schemes of social reform. Moreover, by 1906, the antagonism between Britain's main naval challengers, France and Germany, meant that a combination of the two was, in Asquith's words, 'a myth – not a realisable possibility'. In 1909, under pressure from a vociferous campaign in the Conservative press, the government committed itself to build eight more dreadnoughts. Germany stepped up its own construction programme and undertook the widening of the Kiel Canal, the vital waterway that linked the Baltic with the North Sea. Concurrent attempts to negotiate an agreement on arms limitation with Germany came to nothing.

In July 1911 the naval issue was temporarily overshadowed by a further crisis over Morocco. Following French intervention in a Moroccan internal conflict, Germany sent the gunboat *Panther* to the port of Agadir. The Kaiser's government was prepared to recognise French control over Morocco in return for the concession of territory in the Congo. Although Britain took no direct retaliatory action, a rebuke for Germany came from an unexpected quarter. In the course of a speech at the Mansion House, Lloyd George warned that if Britain were 'to be treated where her interests were vitally affected as if she were of no account in the Cabinet of nations . . . peace at that price would be a humiliation unendurable for a great country like ours to endure'.[1] Although the thinking behind the speech has been variously interpreted, it seems clear that its contents had been cleared with Grey beforehand. The warning certainly served to heighten tension with Germany.

The Agadir Incident had implications of a more practical nature. Since 1906, with the approval of the Foreign Secretary, representatives of the British and French military establishments had engaged in unofficial 'conversations'. These talks now took on a more earnest character, as discussions focused on the question of transporting a British expeditionary force to the continent in the event of a Franco-German war. The wider cabinet was now alerted to the fact of the conversations. Ministers' response was to insist on a strict understanding that no military or naval arrangements with other countries were to commit Britain to war. The approval of the cabinet would be required for any further arrangements. The formation of a Foreign Affairs Group by about eighty Liberal MPs indicated a new determination on the part of the radicals to maintain surveillance of Grey's activities.

German attitudes, however, gave little ground for optimism. Haldane's goodwill mission to Berlin in February 1912 foundered on the German demand that Britain should give an unqualified pledge of neutrality in a Franco-German or Russo-German war. Such a demand not only raised worrying questions about Germany's ambitions but also sought to impose an unacceptable restriction on Britain's freedom of action. The following year Britain agreed to concentrate its naval forces in the North Sea, while the French moved theirs to the Mediterranean. These steps were taken separately and involved a concentration by each country on the geographical area where its interests were most heavily involved. Nonetheless, they were not unconnected. In effect Britain accepted responsibility, morally if not legally, for the defence of the French Channel coast.

Ironically, in early 1914, a matter of months before the outbreak of war, Anglo-German relations seemed to have eased. The naval race had effectively ended and the two countries were able to reach agreement on two outstanding issues: the building of the Berlin to Baghdad railway and the future of Portugal's African colonies. The crisis that drew the great powers into war in the summer originated in the Balkans, an area where Britain had limited direct interests. When the heir to the throne of Austria-Hungary, Archduke Franz Ferdinand, was assassinated by a Bosnian Serb gunman on 28 June 1914, few British people imagined that this would trigger a chain of events leading to a European war. A resurgence of conflict over Irish Home Rule absorbed the energies of British politicians and monopolised the attention of the public.

The Central European crisis was driven by Austria-Hungary's long-standing antagonism towards Serbia, which it viewed as a threat to the security of its multiracial empire. The Archduke's murder by terrorists allegedly linked to Serbia provided a pretext for action. Since Serbia could invoke the protection of Russia, the Austrian government obtained the backing of its German ally before issuing a devastating ultimatum to the Serbian government on 23 July. By 1 August the network of continental alliances had transformed an Austro-Serbian quarrel into a much more serious armed confrontation between Germany and Russia. The pace of mobilisation by the continental armies undermined Grey's efforts to secure a mediated settlement of the crisis. At the same time he resisted French and Russian pressure for a clear pledge of military support. Nevertheless, on 2 August Britain warned Germany against undertaking naval operations in the Channel.

Germany's declaration of war on France on 3 August forced the British to clarify their position. The German war plan, devised years earlier by General von Schlieffen, provided for a lightning strike against France, followed by a movement to the east to meet the more slowly mobilising Russians. Together with Asquith, Haldane and Churchill, Grey was convinced that British intervention was unavoidable. However, he knew that a large number of their colleagues would not take the same view. Many would accept only a limited naval conflict. The Anglo-French entente and the subsequent military conversations did not entail a legal obligation to fight alongside France.

Even if German troops marched through Belgium en route to France, it did not necessarily follow that British troops would be despatched to the continent. Britain had guaranteed Belgian neutrality by treaty in 1839, but under the terms of the treaty, Britain had to be asked by the Belgian government to intervene. If, as seemed likely at first, German troops merely passed through the southern corner of the country, this might not be sufficiently serious to warrant such an invitation. Germany's insistence on gaining passage through the heart of Belgium enabled Grey to persuade wavering ministerial colleagues that the war was now a moral crusade against 'Prussian militarism'. All but two, Morley and Burns, accepted this reading of the situation. The leaders of the Conservative Party had already signalled their support for British action in co-operation with France. It was with a united cabinet, and with considerable evidence of parliamentary and public support, that Britain went to war on 4 August.

Questions

1. How significant was the Anglo-German naval race as a factor contributing to the outbreak of war in 1914?
2. How did Asquith and Grey contrive to take a united cabinet into war in August 1914?

ANALYSIS (2): WAS THERE A REALISTIC ALTERNATIVE TO THE POLICY OF SIR EDWARD GREY IN 1914?

The Liberal government's decision to go to war in August 1914 represented a break with half a century of British diplomatic tradition. By committing herself to fight on the side of France and Russia, Britain embarked on an involvement in continental affairs that had not been part of her practice in recent times. Yet it did not become clear until a late stage in the crisis of June to August 1914 that Britain would take such a step. After a cabinet meeting on 27 July Lloyd George told a confidant that 'there could be no question of our taking part in any war in the first instance. He knew of no Minister who would be in favour of it.' Sir Edward Grey himself told the French Ambassador, Paul Cambon, that Britain was 'free from engagements, and we should have to decide what British interests required us to do'. As late as 1 August the Foreign Secretary refused to give any assurance that Britain was obliged to intervene in a Franco-German conflict.[2] Senior Liberals were keenly aware of their own party's historic aversion to 'militarism' and to 'continental entanglements'. Asquith recorded in his diary that 'I suppose a good three quarters of our own party in the House of Commons are for absolute non-interference at any price.'[3] In the summer of 1914 he and his colleagues were clearly reluctant to contemplate a resort to the use of force. Grey's lament for the passing of the pre-1914 world is well known: 'the lamps are going out all over Europe; we shall not see them lit again in our lifetime'. When congratulated on his success in bringing the nation united into battle, he insisted that his policies had resulted in failure: 'I hate war, I hate war.'[4] Why did this government take Britain to war?

The earliest scholarly attempts to answer this question focused heavily on the evidence of the official diplomatic archives. In the 1920s the British government was one of the first to commission the selective publication of source material relating to the causes of the conflict. Two eminent authorities, G.P. Gooch and Harold Temperley, undertook the mammoth task of editing eleven volumes of *British Documents on the Origins of the War 1898–1914*. In the last thirty years or so, however, historians' attention has tended to concentrate on reconstructing the broader context within which the politicians operated. A range of political, social, economic and cultural factors, bearing more or less indirectly on the 1914 crisis, has attracted scrutiny. Among the issues studied have been the propagation of military values in the Edwardian educational system, the growth of a nationalistic popular press and the pre-1914 craze for novels dealing with themes of invasion and espionage.

Although these investigations have provided many worthwhile insights, it is important, in Zara Steiner's words, to 'show their interconnection and to relate them to specific responses to diplomatic situations'.[5] For example, by 1900 there was a well-established sense of economic rivalry between Britain and Germany, with widespread concern over 'unfair' competition from the rising continental power. With an industrial growth rate double that of Britain, and a significant lead in iron and steel production in particular, Germany seemed a formidable challenger. Yet attempts to use commercial factors to explain the movement towards war founder on evidence of the interdependence of the two economies. In the period 1890–1913 Britain was Germany's best customer and Germany was, after India, the second most lucrative market for British business. Moreover, some of the strongest support for the maintenance of peace in 1914 came from within the City of London, whose prosperity rested on stable trading patterns.

Other aspects of the pre-1914 Anglo-German antagonism should also be examined for their precise relationship with the outbreak of war. In spite of two major crises over Morocco, it does not seem that colonial issues in themselves were particularly significant. In 1911 Grey was prepared at first to press France to reach a compromise with Germany involving Morocco and the Congo. He did not care whether Britain's neighbours in Africa were French or German. What drove Britain to support France was the fear that a surrender to German pressure on Morocco might weaken the entente. It was important to prevent the Germans from driving a wedge between the two Western European partners. The Franco-German colonial dispute was important because of its implications for the balance of power in Europe. Indeed, a year before the outbreak of war the German Ambassador to London, Prince Lichnowsky, reassured his masters that 'no one here wishes to put any obstacles in the way of our colonial expansion and . . . our ambitions are even welcome provided our energy is deployed in the distant parts of the world'.[6]

It is also important to understand the significance of the Anglo-German naval rivalry. Tirpitz's building programme generated a fear of invasion in some quarters. Other sections of the British establishment took the view that the German fleet might be used to 'exert pressure on us at a critical moment when we are involved in difficulties elsewhere'.[7] It was widely felt that, whereas Britain's navy was essential for the defence of a world-wide empire, the Kaiser's forces constituted, in Churchill's words, a 'luxury fleet'. By 1912 Britain had effectively won the naval race. However, its length and intensity poisoned relations between the two countries, contributing to the strong popular support for war in 1914.

The naval issue was relevant to the calculations of British policy makers at another level. Whereas Grey was prepared to be conciliatory towards Germany in other areas, he considered that if 'our Fleet was not superior to the German Fleet, our very independence would depend on Germany's goodwill . . . the Prussian mentality is such that to be on really good terms with it one must be able to deal with it as an equal'.[8] As Paul Kennedy points out, Grey's thinking revolved around the consequences for Britain of a German conquest of France. If Germany overran France or bullied an isolated France into accepting German domination of Western Europe, it would then be able to build up its naval strength and control the Channel ports. Grey therefore considered it vital for Britain to support its entente partner against a German military challenge. British naval strength and the maintenance of a European balance of power were inextricably linked. As Grey told British defence planners in September 1912, 'our concern in seeing that there did not arise a supremacy in Europe which entailed a combination that would deprive us of the command of the sea would be such that we might have to take part in that European war. That is why the naval position underlies our European policy.'[9] The fact that German aspirations to 'equal entitlement' were well known, yet imprecisely defined, increased the anxiety of Grey and of those who shared his outlook.

Grey's concern with the maintenance of entente links earned him the criticism of radical Liberals in his own time. Gladstonian traditionalists in the cabinet mapped out an alternative policy, which involved a search for accommodation with Germany as well as with France and Russia. Lord Loreburn, for example, criticised Grey for committing Britain to a continental conflict and for the secrecy with which he shrouded his negotiations with the French. He argued that the entente would not deter a German attack on France and that Britain's small army would be irrelevant in a land war. It would be far better to concede the German demand for a guarantee of neutrality in a war. This line of criticism has been developed more recently by the historian Keith Wilson in several books and articles. Wilson argues that Grey's fear of isolation introduced a dangerous lack of flexibility into policy making before the outbreak of war. In particular, his concern to reach an agreement with Russia, in order to safeguard British India, involved an unjustified act of faith. Russia proved an unreliable friend in Central Asia and by 1914 serious fissures in the relationship were evident. In Western Europe Grey's cultivation of France encouraged an expectation of military and naval collaboration that was not in Britain's best interests.[10]

From an opposite point of view Grey has also received censure for his failure to turn the ententes with France and Russia into firm alliances. Grey saw his policy of loosely defined arrangements as preferable to the two extremes of outright isolation and of formal treaty obligations to foreign powers. It has, however, been claimed that an unambiguous alignment with Britain's partners could have deterred German and Austrian aggression. Thus the Conservative writer F.S. Oliver argued in 1915 that 'although his intentions were of the best, and his industry unflagging, he failed . . . to adopt the only means which might have secured peace'.[11] The horror of the Great War, and the helpless feeling that something should have been done to avert the slaughter, make such contemporary criticisms understandable. However, they rest on the unfounded assumption that Austrian and German military planners could have been persuaded to abandon their designs. Studies of the decision-making structure of imperial Germany, and of the pressures acting upon both countries' leaders, suggest that there was little possibility of influencing schemes laid in Berlin and Vienna. In the July crisis Germany was unable to restrain its Austrian ally from action against Serbia, and had powerful reasons of its own for launching a war rather than waiting. There is also the possibility that a clear-cut pledge of support for France and Russia might have increased the likelihood of war by encouraging them to act in a more provocative way.

Advocates of a clearer British commitment to intervene also ignore the domestic political constraints within which Grey operated. Unlike his Conservative predecessors, the Foreign Secretary had to contend with a powerful neutralist and quasi-pacifist element in his own party, represented both in the cabinet and on the backbenches. It was politically impossible to move from entente to alliance, as Grey told the French Ambassador: 'should such a defensive alliance be formed, it was too serious a matter to be kept secret from Parliament. The Government could conclude it without the assent of Parliament, but it would have to be published afterwards.'[12] In this respect Grey's semi-committed stance was dictated by circumstances beyond his own control.

Grey himself was privately convinced that Britain could not afford to stand aside in a Franco-German conflict. It was not merely that British security traditionally depended upon preventing one power from gaining predominance on the continent and threatening the Channel ports. National prestige, an intangible yet vital component of great power status, was also at stake. Grey shared fully the analysis of his adviser, Sir Eyre Crowe, who wrote: 'the theory that England cannot engage in a big war means her abdication as an independent state . . . a balance of power cannot be maintained by a State that is incapable of fighting and consequently carries no weight'.[13] The Foreign Secretary's staunchest cabinet supporter, Asquith, was of the opinion that it was dangerous for Britain to neglect her obligations 'in a world ever ready to talk of perfidious Albion'.[14] The consequences of a German victory have already been made clear. If Germany were to be defeated by France and Russia, without British assistance, this could be almost equally dangerous. Britain would be spurned by her former entente partners, and Russia might be encouraged to threaten British interests in Europe and Asia. In the light of these considerations, it is not hard to see why Grey and Asquith could see no realistic alternative to intervention.

Nevertheless, a majority of the cabinet was uneasy about an intervention justified solely on grounds of national self-interest, or of obligation to other great powers. This was where Germany's violation of Belgian neutrality assumed its importance. Abhorrence of such an action provided cabinet waverers and backbench dissidents alike with a moral case for the use of force. The plight of 'gallant little Belgium' did not provoke British intervention, but it ensured that the country entered the war with a united political class. There was a strong conviction that the maintenance of civilised values depended upon upholding international guarantees against lawless militarism. As Michael Brock argues, the deferential character of the Edwardian world assisted the diffusion of this feeling through society.[15]

Few historians would argue that the British government welcomed continental war as a fortuitous diversion from domestic difficulties. It faced a formidable array of problems in the immediate pre-war years, including widespread labour unrest, a violent suffragette campaign and, more seriously, growing resistance to its attempt to grant Home Rule to Ireland. It is true that the Prime Minister reflected more than once in private letters that a European struggle would overshadow the approach of 'civil war' in Ulster.[16] It would be unrealistic, however, to read too much into such characteristically flippant remarks. More relevant to the cabinet's decision for war was the knowledge acquired on 2 August, that the Conservative leaders, Bonar Law and Lansdowne, were strongly in favour of intervention. This meant that if the Liberals' consciences were to prevent them from going to war, they would almost certainly be succeeded in office by a Conservative or a coalition administration with no such inhibitions. Sir John Simon, for example, who came close to resigning as Attorney-General, later said that he had stayed because any substantial number of resignations would have brought to power a coalition government, 'which would assuredly be the grave of Liberalism'.[17]

The Liberal cabinet entered the war with greater reluctance than either the Conservative opposition or the wider public. Throughout the period of Liberal administration foreign policy had been guided by a relatively small number of people, headed by the Prime Minister and Foreign Secretary, whose attitudes differed markedly from those of much of their party. In outlook this elite stood closer to the mentality of the Conservative leaders, who held that 'it would be fatal to the honour and security of the United Kingdom to hesitate in supporting France and Russia'.[18] In line with the received wisdom of the time, they believed that the war would be a relatively short one, following the pattern of most nineteenth-century European conflicts. This expectation, tragically misconceived as it turned out to be, made it easier to accept the fateful decision of August 1914.

Questions

1. 'A combination of self-interest and morality.' Is this a fair description of the reasons behind Britain's decision for war in 1914?
2. Was there a realistic alternative to the European policy pursued by Sir Edward Grey prior to 1914?

SOURCES

BRITAIN'S ENTRY INTO WAR, AUGUST 1914

Source A: Lord Morley recalls a meeting of a group of cabinet ministers on 2 August 1914. The extract is from a book published in 1928, after Morley's death.

It wore all the look of an important gathering, but was in truth a very shallow affair. On the surface they were pretty stalwart against allowing a mistaken interpretation of entente to force us into a Russian or Central European quarrel. The general voice was loud that 'Burns was right', and that we should not have passed Grey's proposed language to Cambon [the French Ambassador]. They all pressed the point that the Cabinet was being rather artfully drawn on step by step to war for the benefit of France and Russia. If I, or anybody else, could only have brought home to them that the compound and mixed argument of French liability and Belgian liability must end in [an] expeditionary force, and [an] active part in [a] vast and long-continued European war, the Cabinet would undoubtedly have perished that very evening.

Source B: Lord Riddell, owner of the *News of the World*, on a meeting with Lloyd George, 2 August 1914.

Lloyd George was in a difficult position. He was bombarded with telegrams from friends like Scott [C.P. Scott, the editor] of the *Manchester Guardian*, who had wired saying that any Liberal who supported the war would never be allowed by Liberals to enter another Liberal Cabinet.

I was told that the Prime Minister was seeing Burns on the following day to endeavour to get him to withdraw his resignation, but that it was doubtful whether he would succeed. Masterman [Charles Masterman, Chancellor of the Duchy of Lancaster] told me at a very critical moment in the Cabinet, he wrote on a piece of paper, 'For Heaven's sake let us all stand together,' and threw it over to Lloyd George. He said that the Prime Minister had acted with great dexterity and good temper, and that Grey had made it absolutely plain that unless France was supported, he would resign. On one occasion he remarked with great emotion, 'We have led France to rely upon us, and unless we support her in her agony, I cannot continue at the Foreign Office.'

When Lloyd George came in to dinner at night he made some reference as to what was going to be done on the morrow. He said, 'We intend' . . . and then added, 'that is, if we are governing the country tomorrow, which is very doubtful.' I said that if Grey resigned, the country would be horror-stricken. Everyone trusted him.

Source C: Lloyd George to his wife, 3 August 1914.

I am moving through a nightmare world these days. I have fought hard for peace & succeeded so far in keeping the Cabinet out of it but I am driven to the conclusion that if the small nationality of Belgium is attacked all my traditions & even prejudices will be engaged on the side of war. I am filled with horror at the prospect.

Questions

*1. Identify 'Burns' and account for the prominence given to him in Sources A and B. [4]
2. Does your knowledge of the 1914 crisis support the view given in Source B of Lloyd George's importance? [4]
3. What evidence does Source B provide of the role of the press in pre-war British politics? [4]
4. How reliable would you expect Sources A and C to be as records of the events of early August 1914? [6]
5. How fully do Sources A to C explain the British government's decision to go to war with Germany in 1914? [7]

Worked answer

*1. [This question requires you to make accurate and concise use of background knowledge.]

John Burns was President of the Local Government Board until his resignation on 2 August 1914. The specific issue on which Burns resigned was the cabinet's decision to close the Channel to the German fleet, which he interpreted as a prelude to British involvement in war. His action was important since he was the only cabinet minister, apart from Lord Morley, to take his unease over the direction of government policy to the point of resignation. The evidence of Source A suggests that many of his colleagues admired him for taking a principled stand. In his deep-seated aversion to war, he represented a widely supported strand of Liberal thought. This explains Asquith's anxiety in Source B to persuade him to stay.

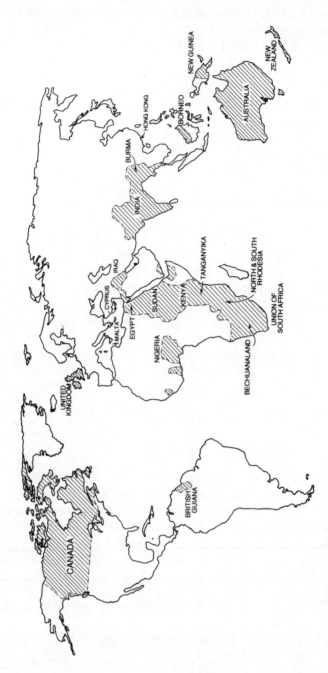

Map 3 The British Empire after the First World War

8

DANGER OR OPPORTUNITY?
The Great War and its impact

BACKGROUND NARRATIVE

Britain declared war in August 1914, not only on her own behalf but as the head of a large and diverse empire. The latter remained a collection of widely different territories without overall coherence: the self-governing dominions, the Indian Empire, the Crown colonies, protectorates and other dependencies. The various government departments whose responsibilities touched on it – the India Office, the Colonial Office, the Admiralty and the War Office – all had different views of the empire and its needs. After the second Anglo-Boer War the Balfour government had created a Committee of Imperial Defence. This, however, fell a long way short of providing a co-ordinated defence mechanism for the whole empire. Nor had any significant steps towards imperial economic integration been taken by 1914. Joseph Chamberlain's proposals for a system based upon preferential tariffs had won support within the Conservative Party but failed to persuade the wider electorate. Indeed, the divisions wreaked by the tariff debate had contributed to the catastrophic Conservative electoral defeat of 1906, helping to exclude the professed party of empire from government for the next eight years. Nonetheless, the empire entered the war on Britain's side with virtual unanimity. Joseph Cook, the Australian Prime Minister, echoed the sentiments of his counterparts in the other dominions when he declared that 'when the Empire is at war, so is Australia at war'.[1] Only in South Africa, where not all Afrikaners had reconciled themselves to the outcome of the war of 1899–1902, did a dominion government face significant opposition to its decision to go to Britain's aid. In terms of the numbers who served in the armed forces during the conflict, the war was a practical demonstration of imperial loyalty.[2] Of the white male populations of the dominions, 13.48 per cent of Canadians served, along with 11.12 per cent of South Africans, 13.43 per cent of Australians and 19.35 per cent of New Zealanders. The Indian Army supplied 1.5 million of its members to the war effort. In all, 2.5 million colonial subjects fought for King and Empire in 1914–18. They saw action in Europe, Africa, the Middle East and the Pacific. The participation of Australian and New Zealand troops in the campaign against the Turkish Empire, for example, ensured that the anniversary of the Gallipoli landings, 25 April 1915, was permanently commemorated as ANZAC Day.

Nor was the empire's contribution to the war restricted to purely military matters. The supply of money and raw materials to Britain was crucial to the mother country's capacity to remain at war. Between the years 1910–14 and 1915–20, for example, the annual value of British imports from Canada increased from £29 million to £86 million.[3] Canada, Australia and New Zealand also helped by bearing the costs of their own armed forces. At the organisational level, the appointment of David Lloyd George as British Prime Minister in December 1916 led to an important innovation in the form of the Imperial War Cabinet. This body, which met in 1917–18, brought together Prime Ministers of the dominions and representatives of the Indian government to discuss common defence concerns. The South African Minister of Defence, Jan Smuts, was a member of the British War Cabinet from June 1917 to January 1919. Such developments raised the hopes of enthusiasts for closer imperial links, who wanted to see more permanent arrangements for co-operation in peacetime.

Other areas of wartime imperial experience presented a less optimistic outlook. Indian nationalism, which had been weakened prior to 1914 by divisions between the Hindu majority and the Muslim community in the north (the area which was to become

Pakistan in 1947), gained popular support as the war lengthened and the imperial power's demands on the subcontinent increased. In response to demands for national freedom the Secretary for India, Edwin Montagu, announced in 1917 that Britain accepted India's progressive development towards responsible government. This paved the way for the 1919 Government of India Act, which enshrined the principle of 'dyarchy', under which elected Indians were to have a degree of influence over certain policy areas at provincial level. Provincial governors were to retain essential powers over finance and policing. Growing unrest, orchestrated by the Indian National Congress Party, led to a return to repressive tactics in 1919. The Amritsar massacre, when British troops were ordered to fire on an unarmed crowd, encouraged a widespread campaign of civil disobedience.

Elsewhere, the end of the war brought worrying signs of discontent with British rule. In 1919 there was violent nationalist opposition in both Egypt and Iraq, which had been transferred to British administration following the disintegration of Turkey's Middle Eastern Empire. The acquisition of Palestine, another former Turkish possession, involved Britain in the difficult task of reconciling the interests of rival Arab and Jewish communities. Ireland, seen by some historians as an imperial issue, was yet another area of concern. Britain's suppression of the republican Easter Rising of 1916, together with her insensitive handling of Irish conscription, had destroyed popular support for the moderate nationalist party. By 1918 the greater part of nationalist Ireland had switched its support to the more radical option offered by Sinn Fein. With its 'military' wing, the Irish Republican Army, Sinn Fein sought Ireland's transformation into an independent republic. Britain thus entered the post-war era with a number of serious problems on the agenda.

ANALYSIS (1): WHAT FACTORS INFLUENCED THE SHAPING OF BRITISH EXTERNAL POLICY DURING THE GREAT WAR?

Britain did not enter the war in 1914 with her strategic aims set in stone. Clearly, the defeat of Germany was the most obvious and fundamental objective. Britain sought to restore the independence of

Belgium and to ensure that Germany was left unable to dominate the European continent. Even in the darkest period of 1917, when the War Cabinet debated the possibility of seeking a negotiated peace, the evacuation of Belgium remained a basic minimum demand for Britain. Other aims evolved in a largely unplanned way, in response to the changing military situation, to the pressures of Britain's allies and dominion partners and to a variety of domestic factors. Two major developments in 1917, the United States' entry into the war and the Bolshevik revolution in Russia, acted in unforeseen ways on British strategic thinking. The collapse of the Russian, Austro-Hungarian, German and Turkish empires in the final year of the war transformed the international situation and brought both risks and opportunities for the future.

There can be no doubt of Britain's determination to break German power in Europe. British politicians associated the final defeat of Germany with the overthrow of the Second Reich's 'Prussian' military culture. This was held responsible for the outbreak of war and was given credence by reports of German atrocities against the civil populations of occupied countries. Political change in Britain during the war tended to reinforce this desire for a decisive victory. Asquith's creation of a coalition government, in May 1915, gave ministerial office to Conservatives, whose attitudes towards war were generally more clear cut than those of the Liberals. This trend was enhanced by Lloyd George's replacement of Asquith at the end of 1916. Britain's new Prime Minister was dependent for his political survival upon the support of the Conservatives. In the General Election of December 1918, fought immediately prior to the Paris Peace Conference, a newly expanded electorate showed its determination to impose a harsh treaty upon the defeated enemy. In conditions of mass democracy the Prime Minister's personal preference for a moderate settlement was overborne by the need to secure a popular mandate.

Although the war was primarily a European conflict, whose outcome would be decided on the battlefields of France and Belgium, the need to safeguard the empire from a resurgence of German power was rarely far from the minds of British policy makers. As the limitations of Russian military power were revealed, the need to provide a barrier against a German overland advance towards the oilfields of the Middle East and the Suez Canal became apparent. This anxiety became more acute in 1917 as revolution in Russia threatened to remove that country from the war altogether.

A subcommittee of the Imperial War Cabinet, chaired by Lord Curzon, warned in May 1917 against tolerating a revival of 'the shattered German ambition of a great Teutonised dominion' extending to Asia Minor and the Persian Gulf. It also drew attention to the strategic importance of German overseas colonies, such as German East Africa, which could be used as submarine bases for attacks on British maritime routes.[4] Security needs thus dictated the long-term retention of territories seized from the enemy in wartime. Moreover, many British politicians anticipated that the defeat of Germany would merely pave the way for a return, sooner or later, to traditional rivalries with France or Russia. In the Far East the need to rely on Japanese naval co-operation during the war obliged Britain to accept an expansion of its ally's power in the Central Pacific region. Britain had to ensure that it ended the war in a sufficiently strong position to resist any encroachments on its vital interests, either there or in the Middle East.

Even had overall imperial requirements not been paramount, pressure from individual dominions meant that the return of captured colonies to Germany was highly unlikely. In the early stages of the war South Africa seized German South West Africa, Australia took German possessions in the Pacific south of the Equator and New Zealand gained control of German Samoa. Each dominion government insisted that its regional security depended on retaining its gains. For all their loyalty to Britain, the dominions were intent on upholding their own distinctive interests. In the words of a report produced in 1917, they sought 'full recognition of the Dominions as autonomous nations of an Imperial Commonwealth', with the right to an 'adequate voice in foreign policy'.[5]

The need to acquire and retain allies outside the empire imposed its own constraints on British policy makers. In order to maintain the co-operation of Russia, Britain had to agree to the Tsarist regime's control of Constantinople at the end of the war. To persuade Italy to join the war in 1915, it was necessary to promise sections of Austrian territory as a reward for fighting. Although Britain had not originally envisaged a break up of the Austro-Hungarian Empire, active support for the subject nationalities of the Habsburg dynasty became a military necessity in 1917–18. The imminent collapse of Russia threatened to give Germany a free hand on the Eastern Front. Britain therefore lent its support to the creation of new Polish and Czech states, in order to stimulate the emergence of armies motivated by the principle of national self-determination. In the longer term this would also create buffer states between Germany and the East, although the durability of these remained an open question.

In the Middle East the war effort against Turkey, which had declared for the Central Powers in October 1914, involved Britain in a series of contradictory promises to other parties. Britain sought to extend her own influence in the region, while conciliating the French, whose suspicions of their ally's ambitions remained unabated. The 1916 Sykes–Picot agreement allocated Syria to France and Mesopotamia to Britain as post-war spheres of influence. Unfortunately, Britain's need to secure the co-operation of Arab groups for the struggle against Turkish occupation had already drawn her into an ill-defined but potentially conflicting pledge. A letter from the British representative, Sir Henry McMahon, to Sherif Husain of Mecca in 1915 had indicated a readiness to 'recognise and support the independence of the Arabs'.

The situation was further complicated in November 1917 when the British Foreign Secretary issued the famous 'Balfour Declaration', in which he announced his country's support for 'the establishment in Palestine of a national home for the Jewish people'. In the context of the war, and of Britain's strategic needs in the Middle East, the declaration was readily understandable. It was intended to rally the powerful Zionist lobby in the United States and to give Russia's large Jewish community a reason to support the country's continued participation in the war. Palestine commanded an important position on the eastern flank of the Suez Canal and it was likely that an influx of Jewish settlers to the region would uphold the influence of their imperial patron. In wartime conditions those members of the British establishment who contended that it would be impossible to reconcile competing Arab and Jewish claims to the area were discounted. Pragmatic decisions, taken without regard to overall consistency, characterised Britain's approach to the region.

Relations with the United States provided another theme of wartime diplomacy. In the first half of the war Britain sought to enlist the active co-operation of the world's most important neutral state, or at the least, to deter it from intervening to promote a compromise peace in Europe. Ties of language, political culture and trade meant that it was never likely that America would join the war against Britain. However, common aims and attitudes could not be taken for granted. It was significant that the USA joined the war in April 1917 not as an ally but as an 'associated power'. American calls for a peace that would enshrine the principles of national self-determination were implicitly antagonistic to Britain's imperial priorities. In order to enlist the sympathy of President Woodrow Wilson, Britain had to tailor her statements of war aims to his liberal, internationalist ideology. Wilson's celebrated Fourteen Points, promulgated in January 1918, included a demand for 'freedom of the seas', a potential source of conflict with a country whose power rested on her naval supremacy.

America's entry to the war was in truth a mixed blessing for Britain. On the positive side, the USA's sheer economic strength, and the promise of American troops for the Western Front, made an eventual Allied victory a certainty. On the negative side, the war provided an opportunity for the dollar ultimately to replace sterling as the world's standard currency. It also stimulated American ambitions to compete with Britain in the provision of merchant shipping. US participation in the war was instrumental in procuring British and French acceptance of an armistice in November 1918, before a crushing military defeat of the German forces had occurred. Had Britain and France elected to fight on, the effort would have exhausted them, enabling the United States to dictate its own peace terms. As Smuts advised his War Cabinet colleagues, by that stage the United States would 'have taken our place as the first military, diplomatic and financial power of the world'.[6] As so often was the case, Britain's wartime policy had to be shaped with an eye to the designs of her 'friends' as well as those of her enemies.

Woodrow Wilson consented to postpone the discussion of contentious issues such as the freedom of the seas until the post-war peace conference. In the case of Russia, however, it was much harder for Britain to contemplate an agreed resolution of outstanding differences. The Bolshevik seizure of power in October 1917 signalled the end of Russia's participation in the war as a member of the Triple Entente and raised fears of the spread of communist ideology, which was presumed by Britain's governing elite to have a powerful appeal to working-class agitators at home and nationalist movements in the colonies. It was no coincidence that Lloyd George chose to make a major speech on Britain's war aims to a gathering of the Trades Union Congress in January 1918. His emphasis on Britain's support for a European settlement based on principles of national freedom and self-determination deliberately catered to radical and labour-movement sensibilities. This was at odds with his endorsement, later in the year, of military intervention in Russia to resist the growth of Bolshevik power. The ending of that intervention in 1919 indicated a realistic acceptance of the limits of British power in the post-war period.

Britain emerged from the Great War as one of the principal victorious powers, with her empire not merely intact but significantly expanded in size. The humbling of her two most prominent rivals, Germany and Russia, by war and internal upheaval, left Britain in a potentially strong position. However, as Britain's wartime experience had shown, the retention of power and influence could not be taken for granted. The rise of Japan in the Far East and the emergence of the

United States as a major player on the world stage were ominous developments. The war represented only a temporary check to Britain's historic imperial rivalry with France. For a Britain economically and psychologically weakened by four years of war, the challenge of maintaining its place in a changing world would be considerable.

Questions

1. How did the changing military situation influence the development of British war aims during the conflict of 1914–18?
2. 'Short-term needs took priority over more long-term considerations.' Is this a fair comment on Britain's conduct of her imperial policy during the Great War?

ANALYSIS (2): WHAT WAS THE LEGACY OF THE WAR OF 1914–18 FOR BRITAIN'S POSITION AS A GREAT POWER?

Lord Curzon expressed a widely held view of Britain's position at the end of the Great War when he addressed a parliamentary debate on 18 November 1918. 'The British flag', he said, 'never flew over a more powerful or a more united Empire than now . . . never did our voice count for more in the councils of the nations, or in determining the future destinies of mankind.'[7] There were many reasons for contemporaries to accept Curzon's interpretation as valid. Britain had played a decisive part in winning military victory and appeared alongside France and the USA as one of the influential 'Big Three' at the Paris Peace Conference. Indeed, with the United States returning after 1919 to an isolationist posture, Britain's diplomatic importance would be further enhanced. The Versailles settlement destroyed German military and naval power and committed the defeated state to the payment of reparations for Allied war losses. Russia's internal problems had temporarily removed it from the international stage. France, the other potential rival for Britain, had suffered enormous physical damage during the war.

Nor were these the only assets of post-war Britain. In 1919 the British Empire stood at its largest territorial extent, with the acquisition of former German colonies in Eastern Africa and of Turkish possessions in Palestine, Transjordan and Mesopotamia (modern Israel, Jordan and Iraq respectively). Although technically Britain governed these areas as 'mandates' on behalf of the League of Nations, she enjoyed all the practical advantages of ownership. As we have seen, the war effort stimulated hopes of greater imperial unity. Lloyd George's governmental changes brought to cabinet rank former servants of the empire such as Curzon and Milner, both of whom continued in office after 1918. At a lower level the new regime advanced the ambitions of imperial visionaries such as Leopold Amery, who moved from being a government adviser on the Middle East to junior ministerial office. Public opinion in Britain was broadly supportive of the idea of empire and, outside the left of the Labour Party, there was no expectation or desire for decolonisation. J.M. MacKenzie's work on popular culture has demonstrated the continuing hold of imperial ideas on the public imagination down to the 1950s. At the end of the Great War, Britain stood on the brink of a new wave of imperial exhibitions and displays, while media as diverse as consumer advertising, school textbooks and the cinema presented the empire in a uniformly positive light.[8]

Nevertheless, a considerable body of evidence can be assembled for a less optimistic view of Britain's post-war prospects. The country's status as a victor in war to some extent obscured the real costs of involvement in world conflict. In order to finance the war effort Britain had been driven not only to borrow on an unprecedented scale but to sell off 15 per cent of her overseas assets, with serious implications for the balance of payments position. The disruption of trade meant the loss of valuable Far Eastern and Latin American markets to Japan and the USA. Perhaps most serious of all, wartime lending by the United States transformed it from a net debtor to a net creditor by 1918. These factors left Britain in a potentially weak economic position when the immediate post-war boom broke in 1920. The ensuing slump had serious implications for a nation whose traditional staple industries – textiles, steel and shipbuilding – were badly in need of rationalisation.

Throughout the inter-war period, economic deficiencies were to place a severe strain on a country with world-wide commitments. Britain's need to defend her own security, together with that of her trade routes and imperial possessions, imposed considerable burdens. Strong domestic pressure for demobilisation had to be set against the inability of individual colonies to suppress local uprisings without assistance from the mother country. The adoption in August 1919 of the 'ten-year rule', under which defence spending was limited by the assumption that there would be no major war in the next decade, indicated the general trend of post-war thinking. In the Middle East the imperial authorities turned increasingly to reliance on the newly formed RAF for low-cost policing of trouble spots.

It soon became clear, moreover, that the self-governing parts of the empire had no intention of subscribing to an overall scheme for imperial defence. Wartime resistance to conscription, both in Australia and in French-speaking parts of Canada, had already indicated that automatic co-operation could not be taken for granted. The dominions' successful campaign to secure separate representation at the Paris Conference demonstrated their determination to push their claims to autonomy. In Kenneth Morgan's words they 'thought hemispherically or oceanically rather than imperially'.[9] For example, Australia and New Zealand favoured the renewal of the Anglo-Japanese treaty, in the belief that its continuation would assist their regional security. On the other hand, Canada, which came increasingly within the economic and strategic orbit of the United States, was opposed to renewal. The consequence of these developments, as Max Beloff argues, was that Britain almost alone had to take responsibility for maintaining the imperial system and for ruling and defending the dependent territories.[10]

Even had Britain's own resources been equal to the task, the post-war climate of opinion was inimical to traditional methods of maintaining imperial control. Public support for the empire did not extend to the acceptance of prolonged and costly repression of resistance movements. The Montagu–Chelmsford reforms in India indicated that the way ahead would lie in an attempt to outflank extremism by conciliating moderate nationalist elements. A similar approach was followed in response to popular disturbances in Egypt. Here the government initiated negotiations with nationalist spokesmen, leading in 1922 to a treaty which accorded practical independence while protecting British strategic interests. Even in the case of Ireland, regarded as an integral part of the United Kingdom, there was no blank cheque for the use of force. By 1921 the Lloyd George government had decided to abandon coercion and to seek an accommodation with the representatives of Sinn Fein.

It is important not to exaggerate Britain's relative decline, by 1919, as a world power. It would take another, more economically devastating world war before British policy makers faced up to a major retreat from imperial responsibilities. Yet for those capable of looking beneath the short-lived euphoria of victory, the situation at the end of the Great War was far from promising. Britain ended the war with a determination to maximise the economic and strategic benefits of her empire, at minimal cost to herself. The attitude of the dominions, and the strengthening of colonial nationalist movements, suggested that it would not be easy to reconcile these imperatives. Britain's war debt and the structural problems of her economy limited her capacity to act as a kind of global policeman. Nor did the United States give any indication of a readiness to share the burdens of maintaining world order. For the first time Britain faced a mismatch between resources and commitments that would ultimately prove to be insoluble.

Questions

1. Was Britain in irreversible decline as an imperial power by 1919?
2. How significant were economic factors in Britain's relative decline as a great power?

SOURCES

PLANNING FOR THE POST-WAR WORLD

Source A: Leopold Amery, a government adviser on the Middle East, writes to the Prime Minister, Lloyd George, 8 June 1918.

We have battled and will continue to battle our hardest for the common cause in Europe. But on behalf of that cause, as well as in the defence of our existence, we shall find ourselves compelled to complete the liberation of the Arabs, to make secure the independence of Persia, and if we can of Armenia, to protect tropical Africa from German economic and military exploitation. All these objects are justifiable in themselves and don't become less so because they increase the general sphere of British influence, and afford a strategical security which will enable that Southern British World which runs from Cape Town through Cairo, Baghdad and Calcutta to Sydney and Wellington to go about its peaceful business without constant fear of German aggression.

Source B: Austen Chamberlain, a member of the War Cabinet, writes to his sister Ida, 26 October 1918.

Shall we have peace with Germany now? . . . I hope so, but I consider that the [United States] President's correspondence has lessened the chances of it. It must be a peace on most onerous conditions for Germany in any case, but I at least would not fight on for vengeance only or even to secure punishment beyond what is inherent in the circumstances of the case – loss of all colonies, loss of Alsace-Lorraine, some losses in the East of Europe, some surrender of battleships &c., a large indemnity. Vengeance is a luxury that few can afford in public or private life. If we fight on, Germany is ruined, but at what a cost to ourselves. Our armies must dwindle; the French are no longer fighting; a year hence we shall have lost how many of thousands more men? & American power will be dominant. Today *we* are top dog. *Our* fleets, *our* armies have brought Germany to her knees & today (more than at any later time) the peace may be our peace.

Source C: Winston Churchill, a Liberal member of the Lloyd George government, addresses his constituents at Dundee, 26 November 1918.

Practically the whole German nation was guilty of the crime of aggressive war conducted by brutal and bestial means . . . they were all in it, and they must all suffer for it . . . Alsace-Lorraine must be completely restored to France. Poland must be reconstituted a nation with access to the sea, and Germany must give up her Polish provinces. None of the German colonies will ever be restored to Germany, and none of the conquered parts of Turkey will ever be restored to Turkey. Whoever has them, they will not. Reparation must be made by Germany to the utmost limit possible for the damage she has done. I cordially sympathise with those who say, 'make them pay the expenses of the war'. If the allies have not claimed this it is for one reason only. It is not physically possible for them to do so.

Questions

1. Explain the reference to the need to 'complete the liberation of the Arabs' (Source A). [3]
2. Which is more useful as evidence of British policy towards Germany, Source A or Source B? [5]
3. What does Source B reveal of official British attitudes towards the United States? [4]
*4. How and why do Sources B and C differ, in terms of content and tone, in their attitude towards Germany? [6]
5. How complete a picture do these sources give of the British government's aims in external policy at the end of the Great War? [7]

Worked answer

*4. The two sources are agreed on the principle of punishment for defeated Germany, and share some common ground in their specific recommendations for the payment of reparations and the evacuation of occupied territory. There are, however, important differences of emphasis between the two sources. Churchill's labelling of the German nation as tarnished with 'war guilt' is absent from Chamberlain's cooler assessment of the situation. Only Churchill uses emotive language ('brutal and bestial') in relation to the Germans.

The context of the two sources may help to explain these differences. Churchill is addressing a meeting during the 1918 election campaign, at a time of widespread hostility towards the defeated enemy. He would therefore use language designed to appeal to the prejudices of his audience. On the other hand, as a minister with governmental responsibilities after the election, he is careful not to demand unrealistically harsh penalties; hence his warning that Germany is not physically capable of bearing the whole cost of the war. The moderation of Chamberlain's comments derives from the fact that he is writing in confidence to a close relation, whose support he does not need to win. He can therefore be more honest in his appraisal of the post-war situation – more so than it might have been prudent for an ambitious politician to be on a public platform.

NOTES AND SOURCES

1. THE PATRIOTIC PARTY: DISRAELI, THE CONSERVATIVES AND BRITAIN'S WORLD ROLE

1. G.E. Buckle, *The Life of Benjamin Disraeli, Earl of Beaconsfield*, London, John Murray, 1920, vol. 5, p.133.
2. Ibid., p.195.
3. See Chapter 3 below for a fuller discussion of this episode.
4. F. Harcourt, 'Disraeli's Imperialism, 1866–8: A Question of Timing', *Historical Journal*, 1980, vol. 23, pp.87–109.
5. N. Rodgers, 'The Abyssinian Expedition of 1867–8: Disraeli's Imperialism or James Murray's War?', *Historical Journal*, 1984, vol. 27, pp.129–49.
6. Quoted in S.R. Stembridge, 'Disraeli and the Millstones', *Journal of British Studies*, 1965, vol. 5, pp.125–6.
7. R. Koebner and H.D. Schmidt, *Imperialism: The Story and Significance of a Political Word*, Cambridge, Cambridge University Press, 1964, pp.109–11.
8. Disraeli to Carnarvon, 20 September 1876, quoted in A. Hardinge, *Life of Henry Howard Molyneaux Herbert, Fourth Earl of Carnarvon, 1831–1890*, London, Humphrey Milford, Oxford University Press, 1925, vol. 2, p.207.
9. W.D. McIntyre, *The Imperial Frontier in the Tropics, 1865–1875: A Study of British Colonial Policy in West Africa, Malaya and the South Pacific in the Era of Gladstone and Disraeli*, London, Macmillan, 1967, p.5.
10. Quoted in Buckle, op. cit., vol. 6, p.382.
11. M. Swartz, *The Politics of British Foreign Policy in the Era of Disraeli and Gladstone*, London, Macmillan, 1985, p.125.
12. Quoted in R. Shannon, *The Crisis of Imperialism 1865–1915*, Frogmore, Paladin, 1976, p.114.
13. Quoted in M. Swartz, op. cit., p.35.

14. Quoted in C.C. Eldridge, *Disraeli and the Rise of a New Imperialism*, Cardiff, University of Wales Press, 1996, p.22.
15. Quoted in Buckle, op. cit., vol. 6, p.84.
16. Stembridge, op. cit., p.138.
17. Disraeli at the Crystal Palace, 24 June 1872, quoted in R. Blake, *Disraeli*, London, Eyre and Spottiswoode, 1966, p.523.
18. R. Blake, *The Conservative Party from Peel to Major*, London, Heinemann, 1997, p.130.
Source A: Quoted in Buckle, op. cit., vol. 5, p.194.
Source B: *Hansard*, Third Series, 1876, CCXXVII, 102.
Source C: Montagu Corry to Lord Beaconsfield, 19 April 1877, Hughenden Papers, Bodleian Library, Oxford, Dep. Hughenden 69/1, H.P.B./XVI/B/22. Copyright: The National Trust.
Source D: Printed in Lady Gwendolen Cecil, *The Life of Robert, Marquis of Salisbury*, London, Hodder and Stoughton, 1921, vol. 2, pp.120–1.

2. LATE VICTORIAN LIBERALISM AND EMPIRE: THE ERA OF GLADSTONE

1. Quoted in M. Pugh, *The Making of Modern British Politics 1867–1939*, Oxford, Blackwell, 1982, p.22.
2. Gladstone to Rosebery, 25 September 1892, in R.R. James, *Rosebery*, London, Weidenfeld & Nicolson, 1964, p.265.
3. Quoted in I. Bradley, *The Optimists: Themes and Personalities in Victorian Liberalism*, London, Faber, 1980, p.136.
4. Quoted in P. Magnus, *Gladstone: A Biography*, London, John Murray, 1954, p.242.
5. W.E. Gladstone, *Midlothian Speeches 1879*, Leicester, Leicester University Press, 1971 reprint, pp.15–17.
6. Quoted in C.J. Lowe, *The Reluctant Imperialists: British Foreign Policy 1878–1902*, London, Routledge, 1967, vol. 1, p.171.
7. P. Knaplund, *Gladstone's Foreign Policy*, London, Frank Cass, second edition, 1970, pp.xii, 19–21.
8. Quoted in Magnus, op. cit., p.287.
9. Quoted in Bradley, op. cit., p.135.
10. H.C.G. Matthew, *Gladstone 1809–1898*, Oxford, Oxford University Press, 1997, pp.350, 183.
11. *Hansard*, Third Series, 1876, CCXXXI, 184.
12. Quoted in Matthew, op. cit., p.186.
13. Quoted in M. Swartz, *The Politics of British Foreign Policy in the Era of Disraeli and Gladstone*, London, 1985, pp.26–7.
14. C.C. Eldridge, *England's Mission: The Imperial Idea in the Age*

of Gladstone and Disraeli 1868–1880, London, Macmillan, 1973, p.86.

15. This work is conveniently summarised in D.M. Schreuder, 'The Making of Mr Gladstone's Posthumous Career', in B.L. Kinzer (ed.), The Gladstonian Turn of Mind: Essays Presented to J.B. Conacher, Toronto, University of Toronto Press, 1985, p.231.

16. K.A.P. Sandiford, 'Gladstone and Europe', in Kinzer, ibid., p.189.

17. As Secretary for India (1880–2) and Secretary for War (1882–5) Hartington occupied a key position in Gladstone's second administration.

18. W.D. McIntyre, The imperial frontier in the tropics 1865–1875: a study of British colonial policy in West Africa, Malaya and the South Pacific in the age of Gladstone and Disraeli, London, Macmillan, 1967, pp.3–4.

19. Quoted in Swartz, op.cit., pp.13–14.

20. Quoted in ibid., p.152.

21. W.E. Gladstone, 'Aggression on Egypt and Freedom in the East', in Nineteenth Century (August 1877), quoted in Matthew, op. cit., p.276.

Source A: Quoted in J. Morley, The Life of William Ewart Gladstone, London, Macmillan, 1903, vol. 2, p.595.

Source B: Quoted in ibid., p.596.

Source C: Quoted in Lord E. Fitzmaurice, The Life of Granville George Leveson Gower, Second Earl Granville K.G. 1815–1891, London, Longman, 1905, vol. 2, p.265.

Source D: Quoted in Morley, op. cit., vol. 3, pp.84–5.

3. A 'NEW IMPERIALISM'? BRITISH OVERSEAS EXPANSION IN THE LATE NINETEENTH CENTURY

1. R. Hyam, Britain's Imperial Century 1815–1914: A Study of Empire and Expansion, London, Macmillan, 1993, second edition, p.104.

2. J. Gallagher and R. Robinson, 'The Imperialism of Free Trade', Economic History Review, 1953, vol. 6.

3. Quoted in Lady G. Cecil, The Life of Robert, Marquis of Salisbury, London, Hodder and Stoughton, 1932, vol. 4, p.310.

4. J.A. Hobson, Imperialism: A Study, third revised edition, London, Allen and Unwin, 1938, p.59.

5. Hyam, op. cit., pp.279–80.

6. Quoted in J.E. Flint, Sir George Goldie and the Making of Nigeria, Oxford, Oxford University Press, 1960, p.273.

7. Cecil Rhodes to W.T. Stead, 19 August 1891, quoted in M.E.

Chamberlain, *The Scramble for Africa*, London, Longman, 1974, p.135.

8. D.K. Fieldhouse, 'Imperialism: An Historiographical Revision', *Economic History Review*, vol. 14, 1961, pp.187–209.
9. A.J.P. Taylor, *The Struggle for Mastery in Europe 1848–1918*, Oxford, Oxford University Press, 1954, p.294.
10. Lord Derby to Lord Granville, 28 December 1884, Public Record Office 30/29/120, quoted in R. Robinson and J. Gallagher, *Africa and the Victorians: The Official Mind of Imperialism*, London, Macmillan, 1961, p.208.
11. Hyam, op. cit., pp.285, 273–4.
12. Robinson and Gallagher, op. cit., p.465.
13. Ibid., p.409.
14. *Hansard*, Third Series, 1867, CXC, 406, quoted in ibid., p.12.
15. Ibid., p.13.
16. J.M. MacKenzie, *The Partition of Africa 1880–1900 and European Imperialism in the Nineteenth Century*, London, Methuen, 1983, pp.44–5.
17. P.J. Cain and A.G. Hopkins, *British Imperialism: Innovation and Expansion 1688–1914*, London, Longman, 1993, pp.351–96.
18. R.E. Dumett in association with P.J. Cain and A.G. Hopkins, *Gentlemanly Capitalism and British Imperialism: The New Debate on Empire*, London, Longman, 1998.
Source A: Memorandum by Clement Hill, 20 October 1884, Public Record Office, F.O. 84/1813. Printed in Chamberlain, op. cit., p.132.
Source B: Sir William Harcourt to W.E. Gladstone, 20 September 1892, Gladstone Papers, British Library, Add. MSS 44202 fol. 229. Printed in A.G. Gardiner, *The Life of Sir William Harcourt*, London, Constable, vol. 2, 1923, pp.191–3.
Source C: Sir Gerald Portal, Report on Uganda, Public Record Office, F.O. 83/1242. Quoted in Robinson and Gallagher, op. cit., p.328.
Source D: *The Economist*, 30 August 1890, p.1109.
Source E: Hilaire Belloc, 'The Modern Traveller', part 6, in *Complete Verse*, London, Gerald Duckworth, 1970, p.184.
Source F: Hobson, op. cit., pp.47–50.
Source G: Robinson and Gallagher, op. cit., p.162.

4. 'THE WEAKEST LINK IN THE IMPERIAL CHAIN': BRITAIN AND THE SOUTH AFRICAN WAR OF 1899–1902

1. Milner, 28 April 1897, quoted in C. Headlam (ed.), *The Milner Papers: South Africa 1897–1899*, London, Cassell, 1931, p.42.

2. Quoted in J.L. Garvin, *The Life of Joseph Chamberlain*, London, Macmillan, 1934, vol. 3, pp.438–9.
3. References are to the following texts: J.S. Marais, *The Fall of Kruger's Republic*, Oxford, Oxford University Press, 1961; A.N. Porter, *The Origins of the South African War: Joseph Chamberlain and the Diplomacy of Imperialism 1895–99*, Manchester, Manchester University Press, 1980; and I.R. Smith, *The Origins of the South African War*, London, Longman, 1996.
4. Milner to Lord Selborne, 4 May 1898, quoted in Headlam, op. cit., pp.234–5.
5. Ibid, pp.288–9.
6. J.A. Hobson, *The War in South Africa: Its Causes and Effects*, London, 1900, pp.240, 233.
7. S. Marks and S. Trapido, 'Lord Milner and the South African State', *History Workshop Journal*, 1979, vol. 2, pp.50–80.
8. P.J. Cain and A.G. Hopkins, *British Imperialism: Innovation and Expansion 1688–1914*, London, Longman, 1993, pp.369–81.
9. N. Worden, *The Making of Modern South Africa: Conquest, Segregation and Apartheid*, Oxford, Blackwell, 1994, p.27.
10. Smith, op. cit., p.403.
11. J.J. van Helten, 'Empire and High Finance: South Africa and the International Gold Standard 1890–1914', *Journal of African History*, 1982, vol. 23.
12. T. Pakenham, *The Boer War*, London, Weidenfeld & Nicolson, 1979, pp.118–19, 122.
13. R. Hyam, *Britain's Imperial Century 1815–1914: A Study of Empire and Expansion*, London, Macmillan, second edition, 1993, p.307.
14. Porter, op. cit., pp.264–5.
15. Edward Hamilton diary, 6 October 1899, British Library, Add. MSS 48675, quoted in I.R. Smith, 'The Origins of the South African War (1899–1902): A Reappraisal', *South African Historical Journal*, 1990, vol. 22, p.39.
16. Lord Salisbury to Canon MacColl, 18 November 1901, quoted in P. Marsh, *The Discipline of Popular Government: Lord Salisbury's Domestic Statecraft 1881–1902*, Hassocks, Harvester, 1978, p.297.
17. R. Robinson and J. Gallagher, *Africa and the Victorians: The Official Mind of Imperialism*, London, Macmillan, 1961, pp.457–8.
18. Porter, op. cit., p.260.
19. Milner to Lord Selborne, 10 July 1899, quoted in Headlam, op. cit., pp.456–7.
20. Quoted in Hyam, op. cit., p.307.

Source A: Lord Salisbury to Joseph Chamberlain, 30 December 1895, Chamberlain Papers, University of Birmingham, JC5/67/35.

Source B: Printed in Headlam, op. cit., pp.245–6.

Source C: South African Government Archives, Pretoria, National Archives Repository (NAR), Non-Public Collection number: A1 (J.C. Smuts Papers), Volume XCVI, No. 5. Printed in W.K. Hancock, *Smuts: The Sanguine Years 1870–1919*, Cambridge, Cambridge University Press, 1962, pp.83–4.

Source D: Printed in Headlam, op. cit., pp.435–6.

Source E: *Annual Register 1899*, p.158. Printed in J. Wilson, *CB: A Life of Sir Henry Campbell-Bannerman*, London, Constable, 1973, pp.308–9.

Source F: Montague White, Transvaal agent in London, to F.W. Reitz, Transvaal State Secretary, 28 August 1899 [copy], Milner Papers, Bodleian Library, Oxford, 19(3) ff.29–30. Printed in Porter, op. cit., pp.235–6.

5. 'SPLENDID ISOLATION'? LORD SALISBURY AND FOREIGN POLICY

1. Quoted in G. Monger, *The End of Isolation: British Foreign Policy 1900–1907*, London, Nelson, 1963, p.17.
2. C.H.D. Howard, *Splendid Isolation*, London, Macmillan, 1967, pp.14–15.
3. *The Times*, 27 February 1896.
4. Howard, op. cit., p.24.
5. Quoted in P. Hayes, *Modern British Foreign Policy: The Twentieth Century 1880–1939*, London, Black, 1978, p.31.
6. J.A.S Grenville, *Lord Salisbury and Foreign Policy: The Close of the Nineteenth Century*, London, Athlone Press, 1964, p.165.
7. Quoted in P. Kennedy, *The Rise of the Anglo-German Antagonism 1860–1914*, London, Allen and Unwin, 1980, p.191.
8. Quoted in K.M. Wilson (ed.), *British Foreign Secretaries and Foreign Policy: From Crimean War to First World War*, London, Croom Helm, 1987, p.14.
9. Grenville, op. cit., p.16.
10. A.J.P Taylor, *The Struggle for Mastery in Europe 1848–1918*, Oxford, Oxford University Press, 1954, p.321.
11. A. Marsden, *British Diplomacy and Tunis 1878–1902: A Case Study in Mediterranean Policy*, Edinburgh, Edinburgh University Press, 1971, p.252.
12. Kennedy, op. cit., p.192.
13. Grenville, op. cit., p.156.
14. Salisbury's confidential cabinet memorandum on 'Anglo-German

understanding', 29 May 1901. Confidential print in Public Record Office, Cab 37/57, no. 52. Printed in G.P. Gooch and H. Temperley (eds), *British Documents on the Origins of the War 1898–1914*, London, HMSO, 1927, vol. 2, p.68.
15. Howard, op. cit., pp. 49–50.
16. D. Gillard, 'Salisbury', in Wilson, op. cit., p.135.
Source A: Public Record Office, Cab 41/20, no.31. Printed in K. Bourne (ed.), *The Foreign Policy of Victorian England 1830–1902*, Oxford, Clarendon Press, pp.426–7.
Source B: Third Marquess of Salisbury Papers, Hatfield House, 3M/D84/29. Printed in Lady G. Cecil, *The Life of Robert, Marquis of Salisbury*, London, Hodder and Stoughton, 1932, vol. 4, pp.70–1.
Source C: *The Times*, 14 May 1898.
Source D: Public Record Office, Cab 37/57, no. 52. Printed in Gooch and Temperley (eds), op. cit., p.68.

6. 'A DIPLOMATIC REVOLUTION?' EDWARDIAN BRITAIN AND THE GREAT POWERS

1. Z. Steiner, 'The Last Years of the Old Foreign Office 1898–1905', *Historical Journal*, 1963, vol. 6, pp.59–90.
2. Quoted in J.A.S. Grenville, *Lord Salisbury and Foreign Policy: the Close of the Nineteenth Century*, London, Athlone Press, 1964, p.346.
3. Quoted in K. Bourne (ed.), *The Foreign Policy of Victorian England 1830–1902*, Oxford, Clarendon Press, p.477.
4. Quoted in P. Kennedy, *The Rise of the Anglo-German Antagonism 1860–1914*, London, Allen and Unwin, 1980, pp.282–3.
5. Quoted in G. Monger, *The End of Isolation: British Foreign Policy 1900–1907*, London, Nelson, 1963, p.281.
6. Quoted in ibid., p.285.
7. Quoted in K. Robbins, *Sir Edward Grey: A Biography of Lord Grey of Fallodon*, London, Cassell, 1971, p.162.
8. Quoted in C.H.D Howard, *Splendid Isolation*, London, Macmillan, 1967, pp.93–4.
9. Quoted in Kennedy, op. cit., p.427.
10. Quoted in M.C. Morgan, *Foreign Affairs 1886–1914*, London, Collins, 1973, p.65.
11. C.J. Lowe, *The Reluctant Imperialists: British Foreign Policy 1878–1902*, London, Routledge, 1967, vol. 1, p.249.
12. D. Reynolds, *Britannia Overruled: British Policy and World Power in the Twentieth Century*, London, Longman, 1991, pp.85–6.

13. Quoted in I. Nish, *The Anglo-Japanese Alliance: The Diplomacy of Two Island Empires 1894–1907*, London, Athlone, 1966, p.242.
14. Salisbury's cabinet memorandum, 7 January 1902. Cabinet print in Public Record Office, Cab. 37/60 no. 3. Printed in Bourne, op. cit., p.477.
15. Nish, op. cit., pp.210, 242–3.
16. Taylor, op. cit., p.400.
17. Quoted in Monger, op. cit., p.282.
18. Quoted in Kennedy, op. cit., p.450.
Source A: Foreign Office print in Public Record Office, F.O. Japan 563 (no. 11A). Printed in G.P. Gooch and H. Temperley, *British documents on the Origins of the War 1898–1914*, London, H.M.S.O., 1927, vol.2, pp.113–14.
Source B: Foreign Office print in Public Record Office, F.O. Turkey 5302. Printed in ibid., pp.298–9.
Source C: Cabinet print in Public Record Office, Cab. 41/30, no. 21, 8 June 1905. Printed in R.F. Mackay, *Balfour: Intellectual Statesman*, Oxford, Oxford University Press, 1985, p.191.

7. 'THE LAMPS ARE GOING OUT': SIR EDWARD GREY AND THE GROWTH OF ANGLO-GERMAN RIVALRY

1. *The Times*, 22 July 1911, quoted in Bourne (ed.), *The Foreign Policy of Victorian England 1830–1902*, Oxford, Clarendon Press, 1970, p.496.
2. K. Robbins, *Sir Edward Grey: A Biography of Lord Grey of Fallodon*, London, Cassell, 1971, pp.291–2, 293–5.
3. Quoted in C. Hazlehurst, *Politicians at War July 1914 to May 1915*, London, Jonathan Cape, 1971, p.33.
4. Robbins, op. cit., pp.298–9.
5. Z. Steiner, *Britain and the Origins of the First World War*, London, Macmillan, 1977, p.3.
6. Quoted in F. Fischer, *War of Illusions*, Dusseldorf, Droste, 1969, p.314.
7. Sir Charles Hardinge, Permanent Under-Secretary at the Foreign Office, 4 June 1909, quoted in Steiner, *Britain*, op. cit., p.51.
8. Quoted in J.C.G. Rohl, 'Von Muller and the Approach of War, 1911–14', *Historical Journal*, 1969, vol. 12, p.665.
9. Quoted in P. Kennedy, *The Rise of the Anglo-German Antagonism 1860–1914*, London, Allen and Unwin, 1980, p.428.
10. See Wilson's essay on Grey in K. Wilson (ed.), *British Foreign Secretaries and Foreign Policy from Crimean War to First World War*, London, Croom Helm, 1987, pp.172–97.

11. F.S. Oliver, *Ordeal by Battle*, London, Macmillan, 1915, p.35.
12. Quoted in Morgan, op. cit., p.79.
13. Sir Eyre Crowe, memorandum of 31 July 1914, quoted in ibid., p.228.
14. Quoted in M. Brock, 'Britain Enters the War', in R.J.W. Evans and H.P. von Strandmann (eds), *The Coming of the First World War*, Oxford, Clarendon Press, 1988, p.146.
15. Ibid., pp.176–7.
16. M. Brock and E. Brock (eds), *H.H. Asquith: Letters to Venetia Stanley*, Oxford, Oxford University Press, 1985 edition, pp.123, 126.
17. D. Dutton, *Simon: A Political Biography of Sir John Simon*, London, Aurum Press, 1992, p.31.
18. Quoted in R. Blake, *The Unknown Prime Minister: The Life and Times of Andrew Bonar Law*, London, Eyre and Spottiswoode, 1955, p.222.
Source A: John, Viscount Morley, *Memorandum on Resignation, August 1914*, London, Macmillan, 1928, p.15.
Source B: Lord Riddell, *Lord Riddell's War Diary 1914–1918*, London, Nicholson and Watson, 1933, pp.5–6.
Source C: David Lloyd George to Margaret Lloyd George, 3 August 1914, Earl Lloyd George of Dwyfor Papers, National Library of Wales, 20433C (1517). Quoted in P. Rowland, *Lloyd George*, London, Barrie and Jenkins, 1975, pp.283–4.

8. DANGER OR OPPORTUNITY? THE GREAT WAR AND ITS IMPACT

1. Quoted in A.J. Stockwell, 'The War and the British Empire', in J. Turner (ed.), *Britain and the First World War*, London, Unwin Hyman, 1988, p.37.
2. M. Beloff, *Imperial Sunset. Volume 1: Britain's Liberal Empire 1897–1921*, London, Macmillan, second edition, 1987, p.191.
3. P. Kennedy, *The Realities behind Diplomacy: Background Influences on British External Policy, 1865–1980*, London, Fontana, 1981, p.166.
4. D. Gilmour, *Curzon*, London, John Murray, 1994, pp.474–5.
5. *Report of the Imperial War Conference, 1917*, Resolution IX, quoted in Stockwell, op. cit., p.47.
6. Cabinet print in Public Record Office, CAB 24/67, GT 609, quoted in D. Reynolds, *Britannia over-ruled: British Foreign Policy and World Power in the Twentieth Century*, London, Longman, 1991, p.104.
7. Quoted in Gilmour, op. cit., p.497.

8. J.M. MacKenzie, *Propaganda and Empire: The Manipulation of British Public Opinion 1880–1960*, Manchester, Manchester University Press, 1984, p.256.

9. K.O. Morgan, *Consensus and Disunity: The Lloyd George Coalition Government, 1918–1922*, Oxford, Clarendon Press, 1979, p.117.

10. Beloff, op. cit., p.349.

Source A: House of Lords Record Office, Hist. Coll. 192, Lloyd George Papers, F/2/1/24. Printed in L.S. Amery, *My Political Life. Volume 2. War and Peace 1914–1929*, London, Hutchinson, 1953, p.161.

Source B: Birmingham University Library, Austen Chamberlain Papers, AC5/1/110. Printed in R.C. Self (ed.), *The Austen Chamberlain Diary Letters*, Royal Historical Society, Camden Fifth Series, vol. 5, Cambridge, Cambridge University Press, 1995, p.97.

Source C: Churchill Archives Centre, Cambridge, Winston Churchill Papers, Churchill speech, 26 November 1918. Printed in M. Gilbert, *World in Torment: Winston S. Churchill 1917–1922*, London, Minerva Press edition, 1990, p.170.

SELECT BIBLIOGRAPHY

PRIMARY SOURCES

Relevant selections of documents for this period are to be found in the following: Kenneth Bourne: *The Foreign Policy of Victorian England 1830–1902* (Oxford 1970); C.J. Lowe: *The reluctant Imperialists: British Foreign Policy 1878–1902*, vol. 2 (London 1967); C.J. Lowe and M.L. Dockrill: *The Mirage of Power: British Foreign Policy 1902–1922*, vol. 3 (London 1972). Dedicated students may wish to dip into the multi-volume official collection of sources, edited by G.P. Gooch and H. Temperley: *British Documents on the Origins of the War, 1898–1914* (London 1927).

SECONDARY SOURCES

For a general introduction, the following are to be recommended: Paul Kennedy: *The Realities behind Diplomacy: Background Influences on British External Policy, 1865–1980* (London 1981); Muriel E. Chamberlain: *'Pax Britannica'? British Foreign Policy 1789–1914* (London 1988); David Reynolds: *Britannia Overruled: British Policy and World Power in the Twentieth Century* (London 1991). Keith Wilson: *British Foreign Secretaries and Foreign Policy: From Crimean War to First World War* (London 1987) contains important essays on Granville, Salisbury, Rosebery, Lansdowne and Grey. The main issues in the history of the British Empire are covered in Bernard Porter: *The Lion's Share: A Short History of British Imperialism 1850–1995* (London 1996 edition) and R.A. Hyam: *Britain's*

Imperial Century 1815–1914: A Study of Empire and Expansion (London 1993 edition). A controversial perspective is offered by P.J. Cain and A.G. Hopkins: *British Imperialism: Innovation and Expansion 1688–1914* (London 1993).

The standard biography of Disraeli remains Robert Blake: *Disraeli* (London 1966). See also M. Swartz: *The Politics of British Foreign Policy in the Era of Disraeli and Gladstone* (London 1985) and C.C. Eldridge: *Disraeli and the Rise of a New Imperialism* (Cardiff 1996). H.C.G. Matthew: *Gladstone 1809–1898* (Oxford 1997) is indispensable. The classic work on the scramble for Africa is Ronald Robinson and J.A. Gallagher: *Africa and the Victorians: The Official Mind of Imperialism* (London 1961). This and other interpretations are conveniently summarised in J.M. MacKenzie: *The Partition of Africa 1880-1900 and European Imperialism in the Nineteenth Century* (London 1983). For the background to the most important of late Victorian colonial conflicts, see A.N. Porter: *The Origins of the South African War: Joseph Chamberlain and the Diplomacy of Imperialism 1895–1899* (Manchester 1980) and I.R. Smith: *The Origins of the South African War* (London 1996). Thomas Pakenham has written two lively narrative histories of key imperial episodes: *The Boer War* (London 1979) and *The Scramble for Africa* (London 1991).

For British diplomacy in the era of Salisbury and Lansdowne the following have not been superseded: J.A.S. Grenville: *Lord Salisbury and Foreign Policy: The Close of the Nineteenth Century* (London 1964); G.W. Monger: *The End of Isolation: British Foreign Policy 1900–1907* (London 1963); and I.H. Nish: *The Anglo-Japanese Alliance: The Diplomacy of Two Island Empires 1894–1907* (London 1966). Paul Kennedy: *The Rise of the Anglo-German Antagonism 1860–1914* (London 1980) is also important. In a class of its own is Zara Steiner: *Britain and the Origins of the First World War* (London 1977). A useful biography of Britain's longest-serving Foreign Secretary is Keith Robbins: *Sir Edward Grey: A Biography of Lord Grey of Fallodon* (London 1971). The consequences of Britain's decision to go to war in 1914 are explored in Max Beloff: *Imperial Sunset. Volume 1: Britain's Liberal Empire 1897–1921* (London 1987 edition). John Turner (ed.): *Britain and the First World War* (London 1988) contains useful essays by David French on war aims and strategy and A.J. Stockwell on the empire.

INDEX

Dominions 95, 100

Eastern Question **3**, 5–6, 10, 16, 62

Egypt, occupation of (1882) 17–18, 19, 23–4, 25, 26–7, **30**, 34–5, 37, 40, 55, 69; rise of nationalism in, 100

Fashoda incident (1898) 56–7, 69
First World War, *see* Great War
France, rivalry with 4, 56–7, 59, 73–6, 79–81, 83–5; entente with **66**, 68–70, 80
Franco-Prussian War (1870–1) **2**, 16, 21, 33
Frere, Sir Bartle 6

Gallagher, Jack, *see* Robinson, Ronald
gentlemanly capitalism, theory of 36–7, 46
Germany, alliance proposals 57, 60–1, 64, 67; as threat to Britain, 69, 73–4, 78–81
Gladstone, William Ewart **1–2**, 4–9, **14–15**, 15–28, 50, **54**, 55
Goldie, Sir George **30**
Gordon, General Charles 18, 35
Goschen, George 59
Granville, second Earl 16, 17, 21–2, 25
Great War, causes of 80–9; impact on the British Empire **91–3**, 93–101
Grey, Sir Edward, Viscount Grey of Fallodon **66–7**, 70–1, 74, 76, **77–8**, 79–81, 81–8

Haldane, Richard, Viscount Haldane of Cloan 74, **77**, 79
Harcourt, Sir William **15**, 38, 71
Hardinge, Sir Charles **67**
Heligoland Treaty (1890) 56
Hicks-Beach, Sir Michael, Viscount St Aldwyn 72
Hobson, J.A. 31, 39–40, 46
Hopkins, A.G., *see* Cain, P.J.

Imperial British East Africa Company **30**, 33, 35, 38
India, importance to the British Empire **3**, 10, 34–5, 70, 84
Ireland 86, **93**, 100

Jameson Raid (1895) **43**, 46, 47, 51, 56
Japan, alliance with (1902) 58, **66**, 67–8, 71–3, 74–5, 100

Kimberley, Earl of 9, 22–3
Kipling, Rudyard 45
Kitchener, Field Marshal Herbert, first Earl Kitchener of Khartoum **45**, 56
Kruger, Paul 17, 24, **43–4**, 49
Kruger telegram 56

Lansdowne, fifth Marquess of 58, **66**, 67–70, 71, 73, 74–6, 86
Liberal Party **14–15**, 22, 85, 86
Lloyd George, David **77**, 79, 81, 87–8,**92**, 94, 97, 99, 100, 102
Loreburn, Lord 77, 84

Majuba Hill, Battle of (1881) 17, **42**, 50
Manchester School **15**, 20–1, 26
Mediterranean agreements (1887) 55–6, 60, 62, 63
Milner, Sir Alfred, Viscount Milner **43–4**, 46–8, 51
Montagu, Edwin, Indian reforms of **93**, 100
Morley, John, Viscount Morley 70, **77**, 81, 87
Morocco 69–70, 73, 75–6, 79, 82–3

Naval Defence Act (1889) 55–6, 60
Navy, Royal 55–6, 59–60, 67–8, 78, 79, 83
'New Imperialism', and Disraeli 7, 11; and the scramble for Africa **29–30**, 31–7

open door policy (towards China) 57, 64